THE NINE EXCESSES OF LOVE

CHRISTMAS NOVENA

BY

LUISA PICCARRETA

LITTLE DAUGHTER OF THE DIVINE WILL

Chi Rho Publishing

CONTENTS

Part I: *The Nine Excesses of Love* Christmas Novena……………………...………………….pg. 1

Part II: Christmas from the Volumes of *The Book of Heaven*………………………………………..pg. 11

Part III: Luisa's Letters………………....…..pg. 77

Part IV: CHRISTMAS REFLECTIONS FROM THE VIRGIN MARY IN THE KINGDOM OF THE DIVINE WILL…………………………………………..Pg. 87

Part V: Appendix……………………………pg. 113

LUISA PICCARRETA

Little Daughter of the Divine Will

CHRISTMAS NOVENA

FROM THE WRITINGS OF LUISA PICCARRETA

Volume 1

Luisa: "With a Novena of Holy Christmas, at the age of about seventeen, I prepared myself for the Feast of Holy Christmas, by practicing various acts of virtue and mortification; and, especially, by honoring the nine months which Jesus spent in the maternal womb with nine hours of meditation each day, always concerning the mystery of the Incarnation."

FIRST EXCESS OF LOVE

As for example, for one hour, with my thought, I brought myself to Paradise, and I imagined the Most Holy Trinity: the Father, sending the Son upon earth; the Son, promptly obeying the Will of the Father; the Holy Spirit, consenting.

My mind was confused in contemplating a mystery so great, a love so reciprocal, so equal, so strong among Themselves and toward men; and then, the ingratitude of men, and especially my own. I would have remained there, not for one hour, but for the whole day; but an interior voice told me: "Enough – come and see other greater excesses of my love."

SECOND EXCESS OF LOVE

Then, my mind brought itself into the maternal womb, and remained stupefied in considering a God so great in Heaven, now so annihilated, restricted, constrained, as to be unable to move, and almost even to breathe.

The interior voice told me: "Do you see how much I have loved you? O please, make Me a little space in your heart; remove everything which is not Mine, so you will give Me more freedom to move and to breathe."

My heart was consumed; I asked for His forgiveness, I promised to be completely His own, I poured myself out in crying; but – I say this to my confusion – I would go back to my usual defects. O Jesus, how good You are with this miserable creature!

THIRD EXCESS OF LOVE

As I moved on from the second to the third meditation, an interior voice told me: "My daughter, place your head upon the womb of my Mama, and look deep into it at my little Humanity. My love devoured Me; the fires, the oceans, the immense seas of love of my Divinity inundated Me, burned Me to ashes, and sent their flames so high as to rise and reach everywhere – all generations, from the first to the last man. My little Humanity was devoured in the midst of such flames; but do you know what my eternal love wants Me to devour? Ah! Souls! And only then was I content, when I devoured them all, to remain conceived with Me. I was God, and I was to operate as God – I had to take them all. My love would have given Me no peace, had I excluded any of them. Ah! My daughter, look well into the womb of my Mama; fix well your eyes on my conceived Humanity, and you will find your soul conceived with Me, and the flames of my love that devour you. O! How much I loved you, and I do love you!"

I felt dissolved in the midst of so much love, nor was I able to go out of it; but a voice called me loudly, saying: "My daughter, this is nothing yet; cling more tightly to Me, and give your hands to my dear Mama, that She may hold you to her maternal womb. And you, take another look at my little conceived Humanity, and watch the fourth excess of my love."

FOURTH EXCESS OF LOVE

"My daughter, from the devouring love, move on to look at my operative love. Each conceived soul brought Me the burden of her sins, of her weaknesses and passions, and my love commanded Me to take the burden of each one of them. And it conceived not only the souls, but the pains of each one, as well as the satisfaction which each one of them was to give to my Celestial Father. So my Passion was conceived together with Me. Look well at Me in the womb of my Celestial Mama. O! How tortured was my little Humanity. Look well at my little head, surrounded by a crown of thorns, which, pressed tightly around my temples, made rivers of tears pour out from my eyes; nor was I able to make a move to dry them. O Please! Be moved to compassion for Me, dry my eyes from so much crying – you, who have free arms to be able to do it. These thorns are the crown of the so many evil thoughts which crowd the human minds. O! How they prick Me, more than thorns which sprout from the earth. But, look again – what a long crucifixion of nine months: I could not move a finger or a hand or a foot. I was always immobile; there was no room to be able to move even a tiny bit. What a long and hard crucifixion, with the addition that all evil works, assuming the form of nails, continuously pierced my hands and feet." So He continued to narrate to me pains upon pains – all the martyrdoms of His little Humanity, such that, if I wanted to tell them all, I would be too long.

I abandoned myself to crying, and I heard in my interior: "My daughter, I would like to hug you, but I am unable to do so – there is no room, I am immobile, I cannot do it. I would like to come to you, but I am unable to walk. For now, you hug Me and you come to Me; then, when I come out of the maternal womb, I will come to you." But as I hugged Him and squeezed Him tightly to my heart with my imagination, an interior voice told me: "Enough for now, my daughter; move on to consider the fifth excess of my love."

FIFTH EXCESS OF LOVE

And the interior voice continued: "My daughter, do not move away from Me, do not leave Me alone; my love wants your company. This is another excess of my love, which does not want to be alone. But do you know whose company it wants? That of the creature. See, in the womb of my Mama, all of the creatures are together with Me – conceived together with Me. I am with them, all love. I want to tell them how much I love them; I want to speak with them to tell them of my joys and sorrows – that I have come into their midst to make them happy and to console them; that I will remain in their midst as a little brother, giving my goods, my kingdom, to each one of them at the cost of my life. I want to give them my kisses and my caresses. I want to amuse myself with them, but – ah, how many sorrows they give Me! Some run away from Me, some play deaf and force Me into silence; some despise my goods and do not care about my kingdom, returning my kisses and caresses with indifference and obliviousness of Me, so they convert my amusement into bitter crying. O! How lonely I am, though in the midst of many. O! How loneliness weighs upon Me. I have no one to whom to say a word, with whom to pour Myself out, not even in love. I am always sad and taciturn, because if I speak, I am not listened to. Ah! My daughter, I beg you, I implore you, do not leave Me alone in so much loneliness; give Me the good of letting Me speak by listening to Me; lend your ear to my teachings. I am the master of masters. How many things do I want to teach you! If you listen to Me, you will stop my crying and I will amuse Myself with you. Don't you want to amuse yourself with Me?"

And as I abandoned myself in Him, giving Him my compassion in His loneliness, the interior voice continued: "Enough, enough; move on to consider the sixth excess of my love."

SIXTH EXCESS OF LOVE

"My daughter, come, pray my dear Mama to set aside a little space for you within her maternal womb, that you yourself may see the painful state in which I find Myself." So, in my thoughts, it seemed that our Queen Mama made me a little room to make Jesus content, and placed me in it. But the darkness was such that I could not see Him; I could only hear His breathing, while He continued to say in my interior: "My daughter, look at another excess of my love. I am the eternal light; the sun is a shadow of my light. But do you see where my love led Me – in what a dark prison I am? There is not a glimmer of light; it is always night for Me – but a night without stars, without rest. I am always awake…what pain! The narrowness of this prison – without being able to make the slightest movement; the thick darkness…; even my breathing, as I breathe through the breathing of my Mama – oh, how labored it is! To this, add the darkness of the sins of creatures. Each sin was a night for Me, and combined together they formed an abyss of darkness, with no boundaries. What pain! O, excess of my love – making Me pass from an immensity of light and space into an abyss of thick darkness, so narrow as to lose the freedom to breathe; and all this, for love of creatures."

As He was saying this, He moaned – moans almost suffocated because of the lack of space; and He cried. I was consumed with crying. I thanked Him, I compassionated Him; I wanted to make Him a little light with my love, as He told me to. But who can say all? Then, the same interior voice added: "Enough for now; move on to the seventh excess of my love."

SEVENTH EXCESS OF LOVE

The interior voice continued: "My daughter, do not leave Me alone in so much loneliness and in so much darkness. Do not leave the womb of my Mama, so you may see the seventh excess of my love. Listen to Me: in the womb of my Celestial Father I was fully happy; there was no good which I did not possess; joy, happiness – everything was at my disposal. The angels adored Me reverently, hanging upon my every wish. Ah, excess of my love! I could say that it made Me change my destiny; it restrained Me within this gloomy prison; it stripped Me of all my joys, happinesses and goods, to clothe Me with all the unhappinesses of creatures – and all this in order to make an exchange, to give them my destiny, my joys and my eternal happiness. But this would have been nothing had I not found in them highest ingratitude and obstinate perfidy. O, how my eternal love was surprised in the face of so much ingratitude, and how it cried over the stubbornness and perfidy of man. Ingratitude was the sharpest thorn that pierced my heart, from my conception up to the last moment of my life. Look at my little heart – it is wounded, and pours out blood. What pain! What torture I feel! My daughter, do not be ungrateful to Me. Ingratitude is the hardest pain for your Jesus – it is to close the door in my face, leaving Me numb with cold. But my love did not stop at so much ingratitude; it took the attitude of supplicating, imploring, moaning and begging love. This is the eighth excess of my love."

EIGHTH EXCESS OF LOVE

"My daughter, do not leave Me alone; place your head upon the womb of my dear Mama, and even from the outside you will hear my moans and my supplications. In seeing that neither my moans nor my supplications move the creature to compassion for my love, I assume the attitude of the poorest of beggars; and stretching out my little hand, I ask – for pity's sake, and at least as alms – for their souls, for their affections and for their hearts. My love wanted to win over the heart of man at any cost; and in seeing that after seven excesses of my love, he was still reluctant, he played deaf, he did not care about Me and did not want to give himself to Me, my love wanted to push itself further. It should have stopped; but no, it wanted to overflow even more from within its boundaries; and from the womb of my Mama, it made my voice reach every heart, with the most insinuating manners, with the most fervent prayers, with the most penetrating words. And do you know what I said to them? 'My child, give me your heart; I will give you everything you want, provided that you give Me your heart in exchange. I have descended from Heaven to make a prey of it. O please, do not deny it to Me! Do not delude my hopes!' And in seeing him reluctant – even more, many turned their backs to Me – I passed on to moaning; I joined my little hands and, crying, with a voice suffocated by sobs, I added: 'O! O! I am the little beggar; you don't want to give Me your heart – not even as alms? Is this not a greater excess of my love; that the Creator, in order to approach the creature, takes the form of a little baby so as not to strike fear in him; that He asks for the heart of the creature, at least as alms, and in seeing that he does not want to give it, He supplicates, moans and cries?"

Then I heard Him say: "And you, don't you want to give Me your heart? Or maybe you too want Me to moan, beg and cry in order to give Me your heart? Do you want to deny Me the alms I ask of you?" And as He was saying this I heard Him as though sobbing, and I: 'My Jesus, do not cry, I give You my heart and all of myself.' Then, the interior voice continued: "Move further; pass on to the ninth excess of my love."

NINETH EXCESS OF LOVE

"My daughter, my state is ever more painful. If you love Me, keep your gaze fixed on Me, to see if you can offer some relief to your Jesus; a little word of love, a caress, a kiss, will give respite to my crying and to my afflictions. Listen my daughter, after I gave eight excesses of my love, and man requited them so badly, my love did not give up and wanted to add the ninth excess to the eighth. And this was yearnings, sighs of fire, flames of desire, for I wanted to go out of the maternal womb to embrace man. This reduced my little Humanity, not yet born, to such an agony as to reach the point of breathing my last. But as I was about to breathe my last, my Divinity, which was inseparable from Me, gave Me sips of life, and so I regained life to continue my agony, and return again to the point of death. This was the ninth excess of my love: to agonize and to die of love continuously for the creature. O! What a long agony of nine months! O! How love suffocated

Me and made Me die. Had I not had the Divinity with Me, which gave Me life again every time I was about to finish, love would have consumed Me before coming out to the light of day."

Then He added: "Look at Me, listen to Me, how I agonize, how my heart beats, pants, burns. Look at Me – now I die." And He remained in deep silence. I felt like dying. My blood froze in my veins, and trembling, I said to Him: 'My Love, my Life, do not die, do not leave me alone. You want love, and I will love You; I will not leave You ever again. Give me your flames to be able to love You more, and be consumed completely for You.'

CHRISTMAS FROM THE VOLUMES

Volume 1

I begin. With a Novena of Holy Christmas, at the age of about seventeen, I prepared myself for the Feast of Holy Christmas, by practicing various acts of virtue and mortification; and, especially, by honoring the nine months which Jesus spent in the maternal womb with nine hours of meditation each day, always concerning the mystery of the Incarnation.

1-As for example, for one hour, with my thought, I brought myself to Paradise, and I imagined the Most Holy Trinity: the Father, sending the Son upon earth; the Son, promptly obeying the Will of the Father; the Holy Spirit, consenting. My mind was confused in contemplating a mystery so great, a love so reciprocal, so equal, so strong among Themselves and toward men; and then, the ingratitude of men, and especially my own. I would have remained there, not for one hour, but for the whole day; but an interior voice told me: "Enough – come and see other greater excess of my love."

2- Then, my mind brought itself into the maternal womb, and remained stupefied in considering a God so great in Heaven, now so annihilated, restricted, constrained, as to be unable to move, and almost even to breathe. The interior voice told me: "Do you see how much I have loved you?" O please, make Me a little space in your heart; remove everything which is not Mine, so you will give Me more freedom to move and to breathe." My heart was consumed; I asked for His forgiveness, I promised to be completely His own, I poured myself out in crying; but – I say this to my confusion – I would go back to my usual defects. O Jesus, how good You have been with this miserable creature!

In this way I would spend the second hour of the day, and then, so forth with the rest – I would be annoying if I told them all. And I would do this sometimes kneeling, and sometimes, when I was impeded by my family, also while working. In fact, the interior voice gave me no respite and no peace if I did not do what it wanted; therefore, work was not a hindrance for me to doing what I had to do. In this way I spent the days of the novena, and when the eve came, I felt ignited more than ever, with unusual fervor. I was alone in the room, and all of a sudden Little Baby Jesus came before me – all beautiful, yes, but shivering, in the act of wanting to hug me. I stood up and ran to hug Him, but in the act of squeezing Him He disappeared from me – and this occurred as many as three times. I remained so moved and ignited that I cannot explain it. But then, after some time, I did not take it much into account. I did not tell anyone, and from time to time I would fall into my usual defects. However, the interior voice never left me again; in everything it reprimanded me, it corrected me, it encouraged me – in a word, the Lord acted with me like a good father, whose child tries to deviate from the right path, and He uses all diligence and care to hold him back, so as to make of him His honor, His glory, His crown. But, oh Lord, too ungrateful have I been with You!

So, from the beginning, the Divine Master began to strip my heart of all creatures, and through an interior voice, He would tell me: "I am all that is beautiful and that deserves to be loved. See, if you do not remove this little world that surrounds you – that is, thoughts of creatures, imagination – I cannot enter freely into your heart. This murmuring in your mind is a hindrance to letting you hear my voice more clearly, to pouring my graces, to truly enamoring you of Me. Promise Me that you will be all Mine, and I Myself will put my hand in the work. You are right that you can do nothing. Do not fear, I will do everything; give Me your will – this is enough for Me."

Now, in order to obey, I will continue what I left on page 6 of this 1st volume – that is, the Novena of Holy Christmas.

3- As I moved on from the second to the third meditation, an interior voice told me: "My daughter, place your head upon the womb of my Mama, and look deep into it at my little Humanity. My love devoured Me; the fires, the oceans, the immense seas of love of my Divinity inundated Me, burned Me to ashes, and sent their flames so high as to rise and reach everywhere – all generations, from the first to the last man. My little Humanity was devoured in the midst of such flames; but do you know what my eternal love wants Me to devour? Ah! Souls! And only then was I content, when I devoured them all, to remain conceived with Me. I was God, and I was to operate as God – I had to take them all. My love would have given Me no peace, had I excluded any of them. Ah! My daughter, look well into the womb of my Mama; fix well your eyes on my conceived Humanity, and you will find your soul conceived with Me, and the flames of my love that devour you. Oh! How much I loved you, and I do love you!"

I felt dissolved in the midst of so much love, nor was I able to go out of it; but a voice called me loudly, saying: "My daughter, this is nothing yet; cling more tightly to Me, and give your hands to my dear Mama, that She may hold you to her maternal womb. And you, take another look at my little conceived Humanity, and watch the fourth excess of my love."

4 – "My daughter, from the devouring love, move on to look at my operative love. Each conceived soul brought Me the burden of her sins, of her weaknesses and passions, and my love commanded Me to take the burden of each one of

them. And it conceived not only the souls, but the pains of each one, as well as the satisfaction which each one of them was to give to my Celestial Father. So my Passion was conceived together with Me. Look well at Me in the womb of my Celestial Mama. Oh! How tortured was my little Humanity. Look well at my little head, surrounded by a crown of thorns, which, pressed tightly around my temples, made rivers of tears pour out from my eyes; nor was I able to make a move to dry them. O Please! Be moved to compassion for Me, dry my eyes from so much crying – you, who have free arms to be able to do it. These thorns are the crown of the so many evil thoughts which crowd the human minds. Oh! How they prick Me, more than thorns which sprout from the earth. But, look again – what a long crucifixion of nine months: I could not move a finger or a hand or a foot. I was always immobile; there was no room to be able to move even a tiny bit. What a long and hard crucifixion, with the addition that all evil works, assuming the form of nails, continuously pierced my hands and feet." So He continued to narrate to me pains upon pains – all the martyrdoms of His little Humanity, such that, if I wanted to tell them all, I would be too long.

I abandoned myself to crying, and I heard in my interior: "My daughter, I would like to hug you, but I am unable to do so – there is no room, I am immobile, I cannot do it. I would like to come to you, but I am unable to walk. For now, you hug Me and you come to Me; then, when I come out of the maternal womb, I will come to you." But as I hugged Him and squeezed Him tightly to my heart with my imagination, an interior voice told me: "Enough for now, my daughter; move on to consider the fifth excess of my love."

5 – And the interior voice continued: "My daughter, do not move away from Me, do not leave Me alone; my love wants your company. This is another excess of my love, which does

not want to be alone. But do you know whose company it wants? That of the creature. See, in the womb of my Mama, all of the creatures are together with Me – conceived together with Me. I am with them, all love. I want to tell them how much I love them; I want to speak with them to tell them of my joys and sorrows – that I have come into their midst to make them happy and to console them; that I will remain in their midst as a little brother, giving my goods, my kingdom, to each one of them at the cost of my life. I want to give them my kisses and my caresses. I want to amuse myself with them, but – ah, how many sorrows they give Me! Some run away from Me, some play deaf and force Me into silence; some despise my goods and do not care about my kingdom, returning my kisses and caresses with indifference and obliviousness of Me, so they convert my amusement into bitter crying. O! How lonely I am, though in the midst of many. Oh! How loneliness weighs upon Me. I have no one to whom to say a word, with whom to pour Myself out – not even in love. I am always sad and taciturn, because if I speak, I am not listened to. Ah! My daughter, I beg you, I implore you, do not leave Me alone in so much loneliness; give Me the good of letting Me speak by listening to Me; lend your ear to my teachings. I am the master of masters. How many things do I want to teach you! If you listen to Me, you will stop my crying and I will amuse Myself with you. Don't you want to amuse yourself with Me?"

And as I abandoned myself in Him, giving Him my compassion in His loneliness, the interior voice continued: "Enough, enough; move on to consider the sixth excess of my love."

6 – "My daughter, come, pray my dear Mama to set aside a little space for you within her maternal womb, that you yourself may see the painful state in which I find Myself." So,

in my thoughts, it seemed that our Queen Mama made me a little room to make Jesus content, and placed me in it. But the darkness was such that I could not see Him; I could only hear His breathing, while He continued to say in my interior: "My daughter, look at another excess of my love. I am the eternal light; the sun is a shadow of my light. But do you see where my love led Me – in what a dark prison I am? There is not a glimmer of light; it is always night for Me – but a night without stars, without rest. I am always awake…what pain! The narrowness of this prison – without being able to make the slightest movement; the thick darkness…; even my breathing, as I breathe through the breathing of my Mama – oh, how labored it is! To this, add the darkness of the sins of creatures. Each sin was a night for Me, and combined together they formed an abyss of darkness, with no boundaries. What pain! Oh, excess of my love – making Me pass from an immensity of light and space into an abyss of thick darkness, so narrow as to lose the freedom to breathe; and all this, for love of creatures."

As He was saying this, He moaned – moans almost suffocated because of the lack of space; and He cried. I was consumed with crying. I thanked Him, I compassionated Him; I wanted to make Him a little light with my love, as He told me to. But who can say all? Then, the same interior voice added: "Enough for now; move on to the seventh excess of my love."

7 – The interior voice continued: "My daughter, do not leave Me alone in so much loneliness and in so much darkness. Do not leave the womb of my Mama, so you may see the seventh excess of my love. Listen to Me: in the womb of my Celestial Father I was fully happy; there was no good which I did not possess; joy, happiness – everything was at my disposal. The angels adored Me reverently, hanging upon my every

wish. Ah, excess of my love! I could say that it made Me change my destiny; it restrained Me within this gloomy prison; it stripped Me of all my joys, happinesses and goods, to clothe Me with all the unhappinesses of creatures – and all this in order to make an exchange, to give them my destiny, my joys and my eternal happiness. But this would have been nothing had I not found in them highest ingratitude and obstinate perfidy. O, how my eternal love was surprised in the face of so much ingratitude, and how it cried over the stubbornness and perfidy of man. Ingratitude was the sharpest thorn that pierced my heart, from my conception up to the last moment of my life. Look at my little heart – it is wounded, and pours out blood. What pain! What torture I feel! My daughter, do not be ungrateful to Me. Ingratitude is the hardest pain for your Jesus; it is to close the door in my face, leaving Me numb with cold. But my love did not stop at so much ingratitude; it took the attitude of supplicating, imploring, moaning and begging love. This is the eighth excess of my love."

8 – "My daughter, do not leave Me alone; place your head upon the womb of my dear Mama, and even from the outside you will hear my moans and my supplications. In seeing that neither my moans nor my supplications move the creature to compassion for my love, I assume the attitude of the poorest of beggars; and stretching out my little hand, I ask – for pity's sake, and at least as alms – for their souls, for their affections and for their hearts. My love wanted to win over the heart of man at any cost; and in seeing that after seven excesses of my love, he was still reluctant, he played deaf, he did not care about Me and did not want to give himself to Me, my love wanted to push itself further. It should have stopped; but no, it wanted to overflow even more from within its boundaries; and from the womb of my Mama, it made my voice reach every heart with the most insinuating manners, with the most

fervent prayers, with the most penetrating words. And do you know what I said to them? 'My child, give me your heart; I will give you everything you want, provided that you give Me your heart in exchange. I have descended from Heaven to make a prey of it. O please, do not deny it to Me! Do not delude my hopes!' And in seeing him reluctant – even more, many turned their backs to Me – I passed on to moaning; I joined my little hands and, crying, with a voice suffocated by sobs, I added: 'Ohh! Ohh! I am the little beggar; you don't want to give Me your heart – not even as alms? Is this not a greater excess of my love; that the Creator, in order to approach the creature, takes the form of a little baby so as not to strike fear in him; that He asks for the heart of the creature, at least as alms, and in seeing that he does not want to give it, He supplicates, moans and cries?"

Then I heard Him say: "And you, don't you want to give Me your heart? Or maybe you too want Me to moan, beg and cry in order to give Me your heart? Do you want to deny Me the alms I ask of you?" And as He was saying this I heard Him as though sobbing, and I: 'My Jesus, do not cry, I give You my heart and all of myself.' Then, the interior voice continued: "Move further; pass on to the ninth excess of my love."

9 – "My daughter, my state is ever more painful. If you love Me, keep your gaze fixed on Me, to see if you can offer some relief to your Jesus; a little word of love, a caress, a kiss, will give respite to my crying and to my afflictions. Listen my daughter, after I gave eight excesses of my love, and man requited them so badly, my love did not give up and wanted to add the ninth excess to the eighth. And this was yearnings, sighs of fire, flames of desire, for I wanted to go out of the maternal womb to embrace man. This reduced my little Humanity, not yet born, to such an agony as to reach the point

of breathing my last. But as I was about to breathe my last, my Divinity, which was inseparable from Me, gave Me sips of life, and so I regained life to continue my agony, and return again to the point of death. This was the ninth excess of my love: to agonize and to die of love continuously for the creature. O! What a long agony of nine months! Oh! How love suffocated Me and made Me die. Had I not had the Divinity with Me, which gave Me life again every time I was about to finish, love would have consumed Me before coming out to the light of day."

Then He added: "Look at Me, listen to Me, how I agonize, how my heart beats, pants, burns. Look at Me – now I die." And He remained in deep silence. I felt like dying. My blood froze in my veins, and trembling, I said to Him: 'My Love, my Life, do not die, do not leave me alone. You want love, and I will love You; I will not leave You ever

Volume 3

December 25, 1899

Jesus wants a continuous attitude of sacrifice in the soul.

After spending several days of almost total privation of my highest and only Good, days accompanied by hardness of heart, without even being able to cry over my great loss, though I offered to God even that loss, saying to Him: 'Lord, accept it as a sacrifice; You alone can soften this heart of mine, so hard' – finally, after long suffering, my dear Queen Mama came, carrying the celestial Baby on Her lap, wrapped in a little cloth, all shivering. She placed Him in my arms, telling me: "My daughter, warm Him with your affections, because my Son was born in extreme poverty, in the complete abandonment of men, and in highest mortification."

O, how pretty He was, with that celestial beauty of His! I took Him in my arms and I clasped Him to myself to warm Him, because He was almost numb with cold, since He had nothing else to cover Him but one little cloth. After I warmed Him as much as I could, my tender little Baby, moving His purple lips, told me: "Do you promise Me always to be victim for love of Me, just as I am for love of you?" And I: 'Yes, my little Treasure, I promise You.' And He: "I am not content with the word – I want an oath, and also an underwriting with your blood." And I: 'If obedience wants it, I will do it.'

He seemed to be all content, and added: "From the moment I was born, I always kept my Heart offered in sacrifice, to glorify the Father, for the conversion of sinners, and for the people who surrounded Me, and who were my most faithful companions in my pains. In the same way, I want your heart to be in this continuous attitude, offered in spirit of sacrifice for these three purposes."

While He was saying this, the Queen Mama wanted the Baby in order to nourish Him with Her most sweet milk. I gave Him back to Her, and She uncovered Her breast to place it in the mouth of Her Divine Baby; and I, clever, wanting to make a joke, placed my mouth to suckle. I drew a few drops, and in the act in which I was doing this, they disappeared from me, leaving me content and discontent. May everything be for the glory of God, and to the confusion of this miserable sinner.

Volume 4

December 25, 1900

The birth of Jesus.

As I was in my usual state, I felt I was outside of myself; after wandering around, I found myself inside a cave, and I saw the Queen Mama in the act of giving birth to Little Baby

Jesus. What a wonderful prodigy! It seemed that both Mother and Son were transmuted into most pure light. But in that light one could see very well the human nature of Jesus containing the Divinity within Itself, and serving as a veil to cover the Divinity; in such a way that, in tearing the veil of human nature, He was God, while covered by that veil, He was Man. Here is the prodigy of prodigies: God and Man, Man and God! Without leaving the Father and the Holy Spirit – because true love never separates – He comes to dwell in our midst, taking on human flesh. Now, it seemed to me that Mother and Son, in that most happy instant, remained as though spiritualized, and without the slightest difficulty Jesus came out of the Maternal womb, while both of them overflowed with excess of Love. In other words, those Most Pure Bodies were transformed into Light, and without the slightest impediment, Light Jesus came out of the Light of the Mother, while both One and the Other remained whole and intact, returning, then, to their natural state.

Who can tell the beauty of the Little Baby who, at the moment of His birth, transfused, also externally, the rays of the Divinity? Who can tell the beauty of the Mother, who remained all absorbed in those Divine rays? And Saint Joseph? It seemed to me that he was not present at the act of the birth, but remained in another corner of the cave, all engrossed in that profound Mystery. And if he did not see with the eyes of the body, he saw very well with the eyes of the soul, because he remained enraptured in sublime ecstasy.

Now, in the act in which the Little Baby came out to the light, I had wanted to fly and take Him in my arms, but the Angels prevented me, saying that the honor of holding Him first belonged to the Mother. Then, the Most Holy Virgin, as though stirred, returned into Herself and from the hands of an Angel received Her Son in Her arms. In Her ardor of love, She squeezed Him so tightly that it seemed that She wanted to draw Him into Her womb again. Then, wanting to let Her ardent love pour out, She placed Him at Her breast to suckle. In the meantime, I was completely annihilated, waiting to be called so as not to be scolded again by the Angels. Then the Queen said to me: "Come, come and take your Beloved, and you too, enjoy Him – pour out your love with Him." As She was saying this, I drew near Mama, and She gave Him to me, into my arms. Who can say my contentment, the kisses, the squeezes, the tendernesses? After I poured myself out a little, I said to Him: 'My beloved, You have suckled the milk of our Mama, share it with me.' And He, all condescending, poured part of that milk from His mouth into mine, and then He told me: "My beloved, I was conceived united to suffering, I was born to suffering, and I died in suffering. And with the three nails with which they crucified Me, I nailed the three powers – intellect, memory and will – of those souls who yearn to love Me, keeping them all drawn to Myself, because sin had rendered them infirm and dispersed from their Creator – without any restraint." As He was saying this, He gazed at the world and began to cry over its miseries. On seeing Him cry, I said: 'Lovable Baby, do not sadden with your tears a night so happy for one who loves you. Instead of pouring ourselves out in crying, let us pour ourselves out in singing'; and as I said this, I began to sing. Jesus was amused at hearing me sing, and He stopped crying; and completing my verse, He sang His own, with a voice so powerful and harmonious that all other voices disappeared at the sound of His most sweet voice. After this, I prayed to Baby Jesus for my confessor, for those who belong to me, and lastly, for everyone, and He seemed all condescending. At that moment He disappeared from me, and I returned into myself.

Volume 8

December 25, 1908

How to make Jesus be born and grow in your hearts.

Finding myself in my usual state, I was longing for little Baby Jesus, and after many hardships, He made Himself seen in my interior as a little Baby, and told me: "My daughter, the best way to make Me be born in one's own heart, is to empty oneself of everything, because in finding empty space, I can place all my goods in it. And only then can I remain in it forever, if there is room to be able to carry all that belongs to Me, all that is my own. A person who went to live in the house of someone else, could be called happy only if he found empty space in which to be able to put all of his belongings; otherwise, he would be unhappy. So I am.

The second thing in order to make Me be born and to increase my happiness, is that everything the soul contains, both internal and external – everything, must be done for Me; everything must serve to honor Me, to execute my orders. If only one thing, one thought, one word, is not for Me, I feel unhappy, and while I should be the master, they make Me a slave. Can I tolerate all this?

The third one is heroic love, magnified love, love of sacrifice. These three loves make my happiness grow in a marvelous way, because they render the soul capable of works which are superior to her strengths, as she does them with my strength alone. They will expand her, by making not only her, but also others love Me. And she will reach the point of enduring anything, even death, in order to triumph in everything, and be able to say to Me: 'I have nothing else; everything is only love for You.' In this way, she will not only make Me be born, but will make Me grow, and will form a beautiful paradise in her heart."

As He was saying this, I looked at Him, and from little, in one instant He became big, in such a way that I remained completely filled with Him. Then everything disappeared.

Volume 10

December 25, 1910

Priests have become attached to families, to interest, to exterior things, etc. This is why it is necessary to have houses of reunion for priests.

This morning blessed Jesus made Himself seen as a tiny Little One, but so gracious and beautiful as to enrapture me in a sweet enchantment. Especially, then, He rendered Himself more lovable because, with His tiny little hands, He took little nails and nailed me with a mastery worthy only of my always lovable Jesus. Then He filled me with kisses and with love, and so I did with Him.

Then, after this, I seemed to find myself in the grotto of my newborn Jesus, and my little Jesus told me: "My beloved daughter, who came to visit me in the grotto of my birth? Only shepherds were my first visitors – the only ones who kept coming and going, offering Me gifts and their little things. They were the first to receive the knowledge of my coming into the world and, as a consequence, the first favorites to be filled with my grace. This is why I always choose poor, ignorant, abject people, and I make of them portents of grace – because they are always the ones to be more disposed, the ones who more easily listen to Me and believe Me without raising so many difficulties, so many quibbles as, on the contrary, learned people do.

Then came the Magi, but no priest showed up, while they should have been the first to form my cortege. In fact, more than anyone else, according to the Scriptures which they studied, they knew the time and the place, and it was easier for them to come to visit me. But no one – no one moved; rather, while they indicated the place to the Magi, they did not move, nor did they trouble to take one step to follow the traces of my coming. This was a most bitter sorrow for Me at my birth, because in those priests the attachment to riches, to interest, to families and to exterior things was so great as to blind their sight like a glare, harden their hearts, and render their intelligence dazed to the knowledge of the most sacrosanct and most certain truths. They were so engulfed in the low things of the earth, as to never be able to believe that a God could come upon earth in the midst of so much poverty and so much humiliation. And this, not only at my birth, but also during the course of my life. When I performed the most sensational miracles, no one followed me; on the contrary, they plotted my death, and killed Me on the cross. And after using all of my art in order to draw them to Myself, I put them into oblivion and chose poor and ignorant people as my apostles, forming my Church in them. I segregated them from their families, I released them from any bond of riches, I filled them with the treasures of my graces, and I rendered them capable of governing my Church and souls.

However, you must know that this sorrow of Mine is still lasting, because the priests of these times have banded together with the priests of those times. They have been holding hands in their attachments to families, to interest, to exterior things, and they care very little, or not at all, about that which is interior. Even more, some have degraded themselves so much as to make even secular people understand how unhappy they are with their state, lowering their dignity down to the bottom, and below the secular themselves. Ah! my daughter, what prestige can their word still have among the peoples? Even more, because of them, the peoples keep deteriorating in the faith and into abysses of worse evils, groping their way in darkness, because they see no more light in priests. This is the reason for the necessity of houses of reunion of priests, so that, freed from the mist of darkness by which he is invaded – families, interest, and cares for exterior things – the priest may give out light of true virtues, and the peoples may turn back from the errors in which they have fallen. These reunions are so necessary, that every time the Church has reached the bottom, this has almost always been the means in order to make Her rise again, more beautiful and majestic."

On hearing this, I said: 'My highest and only Good, sweet Life of mine, I compassionate your sorrow and I would like to soothe it with my love, but You know well who I am – how poor, ignorant, bad I am, and also extremely taken with my passion for hiddenness. I would love it if You could hide me so much within You, that no one might ever again believe that I existed; and You, instead, want me to speak about these things which so much grieve your most loving Heart, and which are so necessary for the Church. O! my Jesus, to me, speak of love, and go to other good and holy souls to speak about these things which are so useful for your Church.'

And good Jesus continued: "My daughter, I too loved hiddenness, but there is a time for everything. When the honor and the glory of the Father, as well as the good of souls, became necessary, I revealed Myself and I did my public life. So I do with souls: sometimes I keep them hidden, other times I manifest them; and you must be indifferent to everything, wanting only that which I want. Even more, I bless your heart and your mouth, and I Myself will speak in you, with my own mouth and with my own sorrow." And so He blessed me, and He disappeared.

Volume 12

December 25, 1918

Jesus repeats His Life in the soul.

Continuing in my usual state, I was feeling all afflicted for many different reasons. And blessed Jesus came, and almost compassionating me, told me: "My daughter, do not oppress yourself too much. Courage, I am with you; even more, I am just inside you, continuing my Life. This is why now you feel the weight of justice, and you would want it to unload itself upon you; now you feel the tearing of the souls who want to be lost; now you feel restless to love Me for all. But in seeing that you do not have sufficient love, you flood yourself within my Love and take all the love that everyone should give to Me; then, releasing your silvery voice, you love Me for all... and all the other things that you do. Do you think you are the one doing it? Not at all. It is I. It is I Who repeat my Life in you. I feel restless to be loved by you – not with a love of creature, but with My own. Therefore I transform you; I want you in my Will because I want to find in you one who compensates for Me and for all creatures. I want you like an organ, available to all the sounds which I want to produce."

And I: 'My Love, there are certain times in which my life becomes bitter, especially because of the conditions in which You put me.' And Jesus, knowing what I wanted to say to Him, added: "What do you fear? I will take care of everything; and when one directs you I give my grace to him; when another does, I give grace to the other. And then, it is not you whom they will assist, but Me; and I will be generous with them according to how they will appreciate my work, my sayings and my teachings." And I: 'My Jesus, the Confessor appreciated very much what You said to me. He cared very much about it, and he worked very hard to make me write. What will You give to him?' And Jesus: "I will give him Heaven as recompense, and I will consider his office as that of Saint Joseph and of my Mama, who, having assisted my Life on earth, had to go through hardships in order to nourish Me and assist Me. Now, since my Life is in you, I consider his assistance and sacrifices as though my Mama and Saint Joseph were doing them again for Me. Aren't you happy?" And I: 'Thank You, O Jesus."

Volume 12

December 25, 1920

The Sacramental lot of Jesus is even harder than His lot as an Infant.

As I was in my usual state, I found myself outside of myself, together with Jesus. I was walking a long way, and on this journey, now I walked with Jesus, now I was with my Queen Mama. If Jesus disappeared, I found myself with Mama; and if She disappeared, I found myself with Jesus. During this walk, they told me many things. Jesus and Mama were very affable, with an enchanting sweetness. I forgot everything – my bitternesses, and even their privations… I thought I would never lose them again. Oh, how easy it is to forget evil in the face of good!

Now, at the end of the walk the Celestial Mama took me in her arms. I was very, very little, and She said to me: "My daughter, I want to strengthen you in everything." And it seemed that She was marking my forehead with her holy hand, as if She were writing and placing a seal on it; then, it seemed that She was writing in my eyes, in my mouth, in my heart, in my hands and feet, placing a seal upon them. I wanted to see what She was writing, but I could not read that script. Only on my mouth I saw two letters which said, 'Annihilation of every taste', and immediately I said: 'Thank you, O Mama – you take away from me every taste which is not Jesus.' I wanted to understand more, but Mama told me: "It is not necessary for you to know. Trust Me, I did to you what was needed." She blessed me and disappeared, and I found myself inside myself.

Afterwards, my sweet Jesus came back. He was a tender Little Baby, wailing, crying and shivering with cold. He threw Himself into my arms to be warmed. I squeezed Him so very tightly to myself, and according to my usual way, I fused myself in His Will in order to find the thoughts of all with mine, and surround shivering Jesus with adorations from all created intellects; in order to find the gazes of all, and make all look at Jesus and distract Him from crying; in order to find the mouths, the words, the voices of all creatures, that all might kiss Him so as not to make Him wail, and might warm Him with their breath. While I was doing this, the Infant Jesus stopped wailing and crying and, as though warmed, He told me: "My daughter, did you see what made Me shiver, cry and wail? The abandonment of creatures. You placed them all around Me; I felt I was being watched and kissed by all, so I stopped crying.

However, know that my Sacramental lot is even harder than my lot as an Infant. Though cold, the grotto was spacious, and had air to breathe; the Host too is cold, but so small that I almost lack air. In the grotto I had a manger with a little hay for bed; in my Sacramental Life, I don't even have hay, and I have nothing but hard and ice cold metals for bed. In the grotto I had my dear Mama who took Me very often with her most pure hands, covered Me with ardent kisses in order to warm Me, soothed my crying, and nourished Me with her most sweet milk. In my Sacramental Life it is all the opposite: I do not have a Mama; if they take Me, I feel the touch of unworthy hands which smell like earth and muck. O! how I feel their stench – more than the manure I smelled in the grotto. Instead of covering Me with kisses, they touch Me with irreverent acts; instead of milk, they give Me the bile of sacrileges, of indifference, and of coldness. In the grotto, Saint Joseph never left Me without the light of a little lantern at night. Here in the Sacrament, how many times I remain in the dark also at night! Oh, how much more painful is my Sacramental lot! How many hidden tears, not seen by anyone. How many wails not listened to. If my lot as an Infant moved you to pity, much more should my Sacramental lot move you to pity."

Volume 13

December 25, 1921

How the Humanity of Jesus was nourished by His Will. The souls who live in the Divine Will surrounded and consoled Jesus at His birth. One who lives in the Divine Will is the closest to Jesus.

As I was in my usual state, my sweet Jesus made Himself seen as a Little Baby – all numb with cold; and throwing Himself into my arms, He told me: "What cold, what cold! Warm Me, for pity's sake – do not let Me freeze any more!" I pressed Him to my heart, telling Him: 'In my heart I possess your Will; so, Its heat is more than sufficient to warm You.' And Jesus, all content: "My daughter, my Will contains everything, and one who possesses It can give Me everything. My Will was everything for Me: It conceived Me, It formed Me, It made Me grow, and It made Me be born. If my Mama contributed by giving Me the blood, She could do so because

She contained my Will, absorbed within Her. Had She not possessed my Will, She could not have contributed to forming my Humanity. Therefore, my direct Will, and my Will which was absorbed within my Mama, gave Me life. That which is human had no power over Me – it could give Me nothing; only the Divine Will nourished Me with Its breath and delivered Me to the light.

But do you think it was the cold of the air that made Me freeze? Ah, no! It was the cold of the hearts that made Me grow numb; and it was ingratitude that made Me cry bitterly at my very first coming out to the light. My beloved Mother soothed my crying, although She too cried. Our tears mixed together; and exchanging the first kisses, We poured Ourselves out in love. But our life was to be sorrow and crying, so I had Her place Me in the manger, to go back to crying, calling my children with my sobs and with my tears. I wanted to move them to pity with my tears and with my moans, so as to be listened to.

But do you know who was the first, after my Mama, whom I called with my tears to be close to Me in my very manger, to pour Myself out in love? It was you – the little Daughter of my Will. You were so little as to surpass my dear Mama in littleness, so much so, that I was able to keep you near Me, in my own manger, and I could pour my tears into your heart. These tears sealed my Will in you, and constituted you legitimate daughter of my Will. My Heart rejoiced in seeing all that my Will had delivered in Creation coming back as whole, in my Will, within you. This was important and indispensable for Me – at my very first coming out to the light of this world, I was to restore the rights of Creation and receive the Glory as if the creature had never departed from my Will. Therefore, the first kiss and the first gifts of my tender age were for you."

And I: 'My Love, how could this be, if at that time I did not exist?' And Jesus: "In my Will everything existed, and all things were one single point for Me. I could see you then, just as I see you now, and all the graces I have given you are nothing other than the confirmation of what you had been given from eternity. And I could see not only you, but in you I saw my little family, which would live in my Will. How happy I felt! These soothed my crying, warmed Me, and surrounding Me like a crown, defended Me from the perfidy of the other creatures."

I remained concerned and doubtful. And Jesus: "How is it? You doubt? I have told you nothing yet about the relations which exist between Me and the soul who lives in my Will. For now, I will tell you that my Humanity lived from the continuous outpouring of the Divine Will. Had I taken one breath alone which was not animated by the Divine Will, it would have been as though degrading Myself, and decaying from my nobility. Now, the soul who lives in my Will is the closest to Me; and in everything that my Humanity did and suffered, she is the first among all to receive the fruits and the effects that my Humanity contains."

Volume 16

December 26, 1923

For one who lives in the Divine Will it is always Christmas, and the mysteries of the Life of Jesus are a continuous act. There are no rags of misery for her. The continuous dying of Jesus, and like Him, of Luisa, in the Divine Will.

I went through most bitter days because of the privation of Jesus. I felt like a most vile rag which Jesus had put aside because it was disgusting to Him, so dirty as it was. In my interior, I heard say: "In my Will there are no rags, but everything is Life – and Divine Life. A rag is torn, becomes dirty, because it does not contain life; instead, in my Will, which contains life and gives life to all, there is no danger that the soul may be torn to pieces, or even less get dirty."

Not paying attention to this, I thought to myself: 'What beautiful Christmas holidays Jesus is making me spend! It shows how much He loves me!'

And He, moving in my interior, added: "My daughter, for one who does my Will, it is always Christmas. As the soul enters my Will, I am conceived in her act; as she performs her act, I develop my Life; as she completes it, I rise again, and the soul remains conceived in Me, develops her life in Mine, and rises again in my own acts. See, then, how Christmas holidays are for those who, once a year, prepare and place themselves in my Grace, and so they feel something new about my Birth within them. Bur for one who does my Will it is always Christmas: I am born again in each one of her acts. So, would you want Me to be born in you once a year? No, no – for one who does my Will, my birth, my Life, my Death and my Resurrection must be a continuous act, which is never interrupted; otherwise, what would be the difference, the immeasurable distance, from the other sanctities?"

On hearing this, I felt more embittered, and I thought to myself: 'What fantasy! What I am hearing is nothing other than a most subtle pride of mine… Only my pride could suggest this to me, and reach the point of making me write so many things on the Will of God. The others are good, humble, and this is why no one ever dared to write anything…' And while I was thinking about this, I felt such pain as to feel my heart break, and I tried to distract myself so as to hear nothing. What a terrible fight, to the point of feeling like dying!

Then, while I was in this state, my beloved Jesus made Himself seen, as though wanting to say more about His Most Holy Will, and I: 'My Jesus, help me. Don't You see how much pride there is in me? Have pity on me – free me from this subtle pride; I want to know nothing – it is enough for me to love You.'

And Jesus: "My daughter, crosses, sorrows, pains, are like a press for the soul. Just as the wine-press serves to crush and peel the grapes, in such a way that the wine remains on one side and the skin on the other; in the same way, crosses and pains, like a press, peel the soul of pride, love of self, passions, and of all that is human, leaving the pure wine of virtues. And so my virtues find the way to communicate and lay themselves within the soul, as on a pure white canvas, with indelible characters. Therefore, how can you fear, if every time I manifested to you my truths on my Will, these truths have always been preceded by crosses, sorrow and pains – and every time, by more intense and stronger pains? It was nothing other than the pressure of the press which I exercised in you, in order to peel you of all that is human. It was my interest, more than yours, that these truths would not mix with the skin of human passions."

And I: 'My Jesus, forgive me if I am telling You this, but You Yourself are the cause of my concerns. If You did not leave me, if you did not hide and did not deprive me of You, there would be no place in me in which to let these fears arise... Ah, Jesus, You make me die, but of a cruel death and of a double death, because I do not die. Ah, if I only could experience death and die, how sweet it would be for me! Ah, Jesus, I am telling You – I cannot take it any more; either You remain with me, or You take me with You.'

Now, while I was saying this, my adorable Jesus clasped me in His arms and with His hands, as though tying me with ropes; and it was as if I were put, pressed – crushed, under a press. I myself am unable to express the pain I felt within me; He alone knows it, who made me suffer.

Then, afterwards, He told me: "Beloved daughter of my Will, look inside of Me, how my Supreme Will did not concede even one breath of life to the will of my Humanity; and even though It was holy, not even that was conceded to Me. I had to remain under the pressure – more than of a press – of a Divine, infinite, unending Will, which constituted the life of each one of my heartbeats, words and acts; and my little human will died in every heartbeat, breath, act, word, etc. But It died in reality – It actually felt death, because It never had life. I only had my human will to make die continuously, and even though this was a great honor for my Humanity, it was the greatest of portents: at every death of my human will, it was substituted by a Life of Divine Will. However, this continuous dying was the greatest, the hardest, the most bitter and painful martyrdom of my Humanity. Oh, how the pains of my Passion shrink before this continuous dying of mine! And only through this did I complete the perfect Glory of my Celestial Father, and I loved Him with a love which surpasses every other love for all creatures.

To die, to suffer, to do something great once in a while and at intervals, is not so great. Also the saints, the good and other creatures have worked, have suffered, have died. But since it was not a continuous suffering, working and dying, it constitutes neither a perfect Glory to the Father, nor a Redemption which can be extended to all. Therefore, my daughter, Newborn of my Eternal Volition, take a look at where your Jesus calls you and wants you: under the press of my Divine Will, so that your will may receive continuous death, just as my human will did. Otherwise, I could not make the new era arise, in which my Will will come to reign upon earth. It takes the continuous act, pains, deaths, in order to snatch from Heaven the *"Fiat Voluntas Tua."*

Pay attention to this, my daughter; do not pay attention to others – either to my Saints, or to the way I behaved with them, which makes you be surprised about the way I behave with you. With them I wanted to do one thing; with you it is something else."

And as He was saying this, He took the shape of a Crucifix and placed His forehead on mine, laying Himself upon my whole person; and I remained under His pressure and all prey to His Will.

Volume 18

December 25, 1925

Disposition is needed in order to possess the gift of the Divine Will. Similes of It.

I was thinking of what is said above – that the Divine Will is a gift, and, as a gift, one possesses It as his own. On the other hand, one who does the Will of God must submit to commands, and ask very often what he must do; he is lent the gift, not to be owner of it, but to do that action which God wants; and once he has done it, he gives back the gift he had borrowed. Many images and similes formed in my mind concerning one who lives in the Divine Will and possesses It as a gift, and one who does the Most Holy Will of God, who not only does not possess the fullness of the gift, but, if he possesses It, it is at intervals and as a loan… I am going to talk about some of those similes.

I assumed I had a gold coin, which had the virtue of producing as many coins as I wanted – oh, how rich I could become with such a gift! On the other hand, someone else borrows this gift for one hour, or in order to carry out one action, to then give it back immediately. What a difference between my richness because of the gift I possess, and that of the one who borrows it!

Or, that I had received the gift of a light which never dims: I would be safe, both at night and during the day, having always the good of possessing this light, which no one can take away from me. It becomes as though a natural part of me, and gives me the benefit of knowing what is good in order to do it, and what is evil to escape it. So, with this light I received as a gift, I sneer at all – the world, the enemy, my passions, and even myself. This light is a perennial source of happiness for me. It has no weapons, and yet defends me; it has no voice, yet instructs me; it has no hands or feet, yet it directs my path, becoming a safe guide, which brings me to Heaven… Instead, someone else has to go and ask for this light when he feels the need for it, therefore he does not have it at his disposal. Not used to looking at all times with this light, he does not possess the knowledge of good and evil, and has not enough strength to do good and avoid evil. Therefore, not possessing the light, always on, into how many deceptions, dangers and bottlenecks does he not find himself? What a difference, between one who possesses this light as his own gift, and one who has to go and ask for it when he needs it…

Now, while my mind wandered in the midst of many similes, I said to myself: 'So, to live in the Divine Will is to possess the Will of God, and this is a gift. Therefore, if the Goodness of God does not condescend to give It, what can the poor creature do?'

In that moment, my adorable Jesus moved in my interior, as though squeezing me all to Himself, and told me: "My daughter, it is true that to live in my Will is a gift, and it is to possess the greatest gift. However, this gift – which contains infinite value, which is currency coined in every instant, which is light that never dims, which is Sun that never sets, which puts the soul in her place, established by God in the divine order, therefore taking her place of honor and sovereignty in the Creation – is given only to one who is disposed, to one who will not waste it, to one who will esteem it and love it more than her own life; so much so, as to be able to sacrifice her life, in order to let this gift of my Will have supremacy over all, and to be taken into consideration more than life itself – even more, that her own life be nothing compared to It.

Therefore, first I want to see that the soul really wants to do my Will and never her own, that she is ready to make any sacrifice in order to do Mine, and that in everything she does, she always asks Me for the gift of my Will, even just as a loan.

When I see that she does nothing without the loan my Will, I give It to her as a gift, because by asking for It over and over again, she has formed the void in her soul, in which to place this celestial gift; and by getting used to living with the loan of this divine Food, she has lost the taste for her own will; her palate has been ennobled and will no longer adapt itself to the vile food of her own self. Therefore, in seeing that she possesses that gift which she longed for, yearned for, and loved so much, she will live from the life of that gift, she will love It and esteem It as It deserves.

Would you not condemn a man, who, taken with a childish affection for a little boy – only to have him around a little to amuse himself with him – would give him a banknote worth a thousand; and the child, not knowing its value, tears it to a thousand pieces after a few minutes? But if, instead, he makes the child desire it first, then he makes him know its value, then the good which that banknote of a thousand could do for him, and then gives it to him – that child would not tear it to pieces, but would go put it under lock and key, appreciating the gift and loving the giver more; and you would praise that man who had the ability to make known to the little boy the value of the money… If man does so, much more do I, Who give my gifts with wisdom, with justice and with true love. Here is, therefore, the necessity of disposition, of the knowledge of the gift, of esteem and appreciation, and of love for the gift itself.

Therefore, knowledge of It is like the bearer of the gift of my Will which I want to give to the creature. Knowledge prepares the way. Knowledge is like the contract I want to make of the gift I want to give. And the more knowledge I send to the soul, the more she is spurred on to desire the gift and to solicit the Divine Writer to place the final signature – that the gift is hers and she possesses it. So, the sign that in these times I want to give this gift of my Will, is the knowledge of It. Therefore, be attentive not to let anything escape you of what I manifest to you about my Will, if you want Me to place the final signature on the gift which I yearn to give to the creatures."

After this, my poor mind dissolved in the Supreme Volition, and I did as much as I could in order to do all my acts in the Divine Volition. I felt invested with a supreme light, and as my little acts came out of myself, they took their place in that light and were converted into light; and I could see neither the point of light at which I had done them, nor where to find them. I could only see that they had become part of that light and could no longer be seen. It was impossible for me to navigate through all that inaccessible light: to remain inside of It, yes, but crossing It was not allowed to my littleness.

In the meantime, my adorable Jesus moved in my interior and told me: "My daughter, how beautiful are the works of the soul in my Will! Her act unites to the single Act of her Creator, which does not know succession of acts, because eternal Light is not divisible, and if it could be divided – which cannot be – the divided part would become darkness. Therefore, since the divine Act is light of all her works, It forms one single act. Operating in the Light of my Volition, the soul unites to that single Act of her Creator and takes her place within the sphere of the Eternal Light. This is why you cannot see your acts, either in the point of Light where you performed them, or where they are now: because it is impossible for the creature to cross the eternal Light of God completely, although she knows that her act is certainly present in that Light, and takes its place in the past, in the present, and in the future.

See, the Sun too has, in part, this property, being image and shadow of the divine Light. Suppose you were operating at a point on which the Sun spreads its solar light: you see its light in front of you, above and behind you, on the right and on the left. If you wanted to see which was the part of the light of the Sun that surrounded you completely, you would not be able to find it, or distinguish it; you could only say that the light was certainly on you. Now, that light has been, since the first instant in which the Sun was created; and it is and will be. If your act could convert into solar light as it converts into divine Light, could you perhaps find your little particle of light, and the light which was given to you by the Sun in order to let you operate? Certainly not. However, you know that an act came from you, which was incorporated into the light of the Sun. This is why I say that to live in the Supreme Volition is the greatest thing – it is to live Divine Life.

As soon as He sees the soul in His Will, the Celestial Creator takes her in His arms, and placing her on His lap, lets her operate with His own hands, and with the power of that FIAT through which all things were created. He lets all His reflections descend upon the creature, in order to give her the likeness of His works. This is why the work of the creature becomes light, unites to that single Act of her Creator, and becomes eternal glory and continuous praise to her Creator. Therefore, be attentive, and let the living in my Will be your All.

Volume 20

December 25, 1926

How the Little Baby made Himself seen, newly born, by His Mama. The light which the Little Baby sent forth, greeting everyone at His coming upon earth. Difference between the grotto and the prison of the Passion.

I was anxiously waiting for little Baby Jesus, and after many sighs, finally He came; and throwing Himself into my arms, as a little baby, He said to me: "My daughter, do you want to see how my inseparable Mama saw Me, when I came out of Her Maternal womb? Look at Me, and see."

I looked at Him, and I saw Him as a little baby, of rare and enrapturing beauty. From all of His little Humanity, from His eyes, from His mouth, from His hands and feet, came most refulgent rays of light, which not only enwrapped Him, but extended so much as to be able to wound each heart of creature, almost to give her the first greeting of His coming upon earth – the first knock to knock at hearts, to make them open and to ask for a shelter within them. That knock was sweet but penetrating; however, being a knock of light, it made no clamor, yet, it made itself be heard strongly, more than any noise. So, on that night, all felt something unusual within their hearts, but very few were those who opened their hearts to give

Him a little shelter. And the tender infant, in feeling His greeting not being returned, and that no one opened at His repeated knocking, began His crying. With His lips livid and shivering with cold, He sobbed, wailed and sighed. But while the light which came from Him was doing all this with the creatures, receiving the first rejections, as He came out of the womb of His Celestial Mama, He threw Himself into Her maternal arms to give Her the first hug, the first kiss. And since His little arms could not reach to embrace Her completely, the light which came out of His little hands surrounded all of Her, in such a way that Mother and Son remained invested with the same light. O! how the Queen Mama requited Her Son with Her embrace and kiss; in such a way that they remained so clasped to each other as to seem to be fused within each other. With Her love, She compensated for the first rejection which Jesus received from the hearts of the creatures, and the dear and charming little baby placed His first act of being born, His graces, His first sorrow, into the heart of His Mama, so that what appeared in the Son could appear in the Mother.

After this, the gracious little baby came into my arms, and as He squeezed me very tightly, I felt He was entering into me, and I into Him. Then He said to me: "My daughter, I wanted to hug you as I hugged my dear Mama as newly born, so that you too may receive my first act of being born and my first sorrow, my tears, my tender wailings, that you may be moved to compassion for my sorrowful state at my birth. Had I not had my Mama in whom to place all the good of my birth and to fix the light of my Divinity which I, Word of the Father, contained, I would have found no one in whom either to place the infinite treasure of my birth, or to fix the light of my Divinity which shone forth from my Humanity. Therefore, see how necessary it is that, when the Supreme Majesty decides to do a great good for the creatures, which can serve as universal good, We choose one to whom to give so much grace that she may be able to receive within her all the good that all the others must receive. In fact, if the others do not receive all of it or part of it, Our work does not remain suspended and without its fruit, but the chosen soul receives all of that good within her, and Our work receives the return of its fruit.

So, my Mama was the depository, not only of my life, but of all my acts. Therefore, in all of my acts, first I looked to see whether I could deposit them in Her, and then I did them. In Her I deposited my tears, my wailings, the cold and the pains I suffered; and She echoed all of my acts, and with incessant thanksgivings, She received everything. There was a contest between Mother and Son – I in giving, She in receiving. As my little Humanity made Its first entrance on earth, my Divinity wanted to shine forth from It, in order to go around everywhere and to make the first sensible visit to all Creation. Heaven and earth – all received this visit of their Creator, except for man. They had never received so much honor and glory as when they saw their King, their Maker, within their midst; all felt honored in having to serve the One from whom they had received their existence, therefore all made feast. So, my birth was of great joy and glory for Me on the part of my Mama and of all Creation; but it was a great sorrow on the part of creatures. This is why I have come to you – to feel the joys of my Mama being repeated, and to place in you the fruit of my birth."

Then, after this, I was thinking of how unhappy was that grotto in which little baby Jesus was born; how exposed it was to all winds and to cold, so much as to make one numb with cold. Instead of men, there were animals which kept Him company. So I thought: 'Which prison was more unhappy and sorrowful – the prison of the night of His Passion, or the grotto of Bethlehem?' And my sweet baby added: "My daughter, the unhappiness of the prison of my Passion cannot be compared to the grotto of Bethlehem. In the grotto I had my Mama near Me, in body and soul. She was with Me, therefore I had all the joys of my dear Mama, and She had all the joys of Myself, Her Son, which formed our Paradise. The joys of a Mother who possesses her child are great; the joys of possessing a Mother are even greater. I found everything in Her, and She found everything in Me. Then there was my dear father Saint Joseph who acted as a father to Me, and I felt all the joys which he felt because of Me. In my Passion, instead, all of our joys were interrupted, because we were to give place to sorrow, and between Mother and Son, we felt the great pain of the nearing separation, sensible at least, which was to occur with my death. In the grotto the animals recognized Me, and honoring Me, they tried to warm Me with their breath. In the prison, not even men recognized Me, and in order to insult Me, they covered Me with spit and opprobrium. So, there is no comparison between the two."

Volume 20

January 1, 1927

The will of the soul as a Christmas gift for Baby Jesus. How all of His life was a symbol and a call of the Divine Will. The knowledges are the means in order to hasten the coming of the Kingdom of His Will.

I was meditating on the old year which was setting, and the new one which was rising. My state continued in the flight of the light of the Divine Will, and I prayed the pretty Little Baby that, just as the old year was dying never to be born again, He would make my will die and live no more; and as gift for the new year, He would give me His Will, just as I gave Him mine as gift, placing it as footstool at His tender little feet, that it might have no life but His Will alone. Now, while I was saying these and other things, my sweet Jesus came out from within my interior, and told me: "Daughter of my Will, how I love, want and yearn that your will may end in you. O, how I accept your gift! How pleasing it will be for Me to keep it at my feet as a soft footstool. In fact, as long as it remains in the creature, outside of its center, which is God, the human will is hard; but when it enters once again into the center from which it came, serving as footstool at the feet of its Little Baby Jesus, it becomes soft, and I use it to amuse Myself. Is it not fair that, being little, I have my amusement? And that in the midst of so many sorrows, privations and tears, I may hold your will to make Me smile? Now, you must know that one who puts an end to his will, returns to the origin from which he came, and the new life, the life of light, the perennial life of my Will, begins in him.

See, when I came upon earth, I wanted to give many examples and similes about how I wanted the human will to end. I wanted to be born at midnight, so as to break the night of the human will with the refulgent day of Mine. And even though at midnight the night continues and does not finish, it is yet the beginning of a new day; and my Angels, to honor my birth and to point out to everyone the day of my Will, from midnight on, enlivened the vault of the heavens with new stars and new suns, such as to turn the night into more than daylight. This was the homage that the Angels gave to my little Humanity, in which dwelled the full day of the sun of my Divine Will, and the call of the creature into the full day of It. Still little, I submitted Myself to the cruel cut of circumcision, which made Me shed bitter tears for the pain – and not only to Me, but with Me cried my Mama and dear St. Joseph. It was the cut of the human will that I wanted to make, so that all might let the Divine Will flow within that cut, and so that a broken will might have life no more – but only Mine, which had flowed within that cut in order to begin Its life again.

Still little, I wanted to flee to Egypt. A tyrannical and iniquitous will wanted to kill Me – symbol of the human will which wants to kill Mine; so I fled, in order to say to all: 'Flee the human will, if you do not want Mine to be killed.' My whole life was nothing other than the call of the Divine Will into the human. In Egypt I lived like a stranger in the midst of that people – symbol of my Will, which they keep as though estranged within their midst; and symbolizing that whoever wants to live in peace and united with my Will, must live as though estranged to the human will. Otherwise, there will always be war between the two of them, because they are two irreconcilable wills.

After my exile, I returned to my fatherland – symbol of my Will which, after Its long exile of centuries upon centuries, will return to Its dear fatherland, to reign in the midst of Its children. And as I went through these stages in my life, I kept forming Its Kingdom in Me, and I called It with incessant prayers, with pains and with tears, to come and reign in the midst of creatures. I returned to my fatherland and I lived hidden and unknown. O, how this symbolizes the sorrow of my Will which, while living in the midst of the peoples, lives unknown and hidden! And with my hiddenness, I impetrated that the Supreme Will might be known, in order to receive the homage and the glory which are due to It.

There was nothing I did which did not symbolize a sorrow of my Will, the condition in which creatures put It, and the call I made in order to return Its Kingdom to It. And this is what I want your life to be: the continuous call of the Kingdom of my Will into the midst of creatures."

Then, after this, I was going around throughout the whole Creation in order to bring the heavens, the stars, the sun, the moon, the sea – in sum, everything, to the feet of Little Baby Jesus together with me, to ask Him, all together, that this Kingdom of His Will may come soon upon earth. And in my desire, I said: 'See, I am not the only one who is praying You, but the heavens are praying with the voices of all the stars; the sun, with the voice of its light and of its heat, the sea with its murmuring – they are all praying that your Will may come to reign upon earth. How can You resist listening to so many voices that pray You? They are innocent voices – voices animated by your own Will, that are praying You.'

Now, while I was saying this, my little Jesus came out from within my interior to receive the homage of all Creation, and to listen to their mute language; and squeezing me to Himself, He told me: "My daughter, the easiest means in order to hasten the coming of my Will upon earth are the knowledges about It. The knowledges bring light and heat and form the prime act of God within themselves, in which the creature finds the prime act on which to model her own. If she does not find the first act, the creature does not have the virtue of forming the prime act; therefore the acts and the things which are most necessary in order to form this Kingdom, would be missing. See then, what one additional knowledge about my Will means. By carrying the prime act of God within itself, it brings with itself a magnetic force– a powerful magnet in order to draw the creatures to repeating the prime act of God. With its light, it will bring the disillusionment of the human will; with its heat, it will soften the hardest hearts, moving them to bend before these Divine acts; and they will feel enraptured, yearning to be modeled on this act. Therefore, the more knowledges I manifest about my Will, the more the Kingdom of the Divine Fiat will hasten Its coming upon earth."

Volume 23

December 25, 1927

How Baby Jesus, newly born, fixes His gaze on His Mama and on the one who was to possess His Will. How, in Creation, God placed His Will as raw material.

I was feeling all abandoned in the Supreme Volition, but all tormented by the total privation of my sweet Jesus. Oh! how I felt my poor soul being torn to pieces. What tearings without mercy and without pity, because the One who alone can heal tearings so cruel is far away, and seems not to care about the one who, for love of Him, is so cruelly tormented. But while I was swimming in my sorrow, I was thinking of when my sweet Jesus was about to come out of the womb of His beloved Mama to fling Himself into Her arms. Oh! how I too would have wanted to squeeze Him in my arms, to form sweet chains for Him, so that He might no longer depart from me. But while I was thinking of this, I felt my poor mind outside of myself, and I saw my Celestial Mama, all veiled with light, and, in Her arms, little Baby Jesus, fused in the same light. But it lasted only a few instants, and then everything disappeared, and I remained more afflicted than before. However, later He came back, and clasping His little hands around my neck, He told me: "My daughter, as soon as I came out of the womb of my Mama, I fixed my gazes – one on my dear Mama; nor could I do without looking at Her, because in Her was the enrapturing force of the Divine Will and the sweet enchantment of the beauty and most refulgent light of my Fiat which, eclipsing my pupil, made Me remain fixed in She who possessed my very life by virtue of It. Seeing my life bilocated in Her enraptured Me, and I could not remove my gaze from the Celestial Queen, because my very divine force compelled Me to fix on Her. The other gaze I fixed on the one who was to do and possess my

Will. They were two links connected together – the Redemption and the Kingdom of my Divine Will – inseparable from each other. The Redemption was to prepare, suffer, do; the Kingdom of the Fiat was to fulfill and possess – both of them of highest importance. Therefore, my gazes were fixed on the chosen ones to whom both one and the other were entrusted, because there was my very Will in them that enraptured my pupil. Why do you fear, then, if you have the gaze of your Jesus always looking at you, defending you, protecting you? If you knew what it means to be looked upon by Me, you would no longer fear anything."

Then, afterwards, I continued to think about the Divine Will; and my always lovable Jesus added: "My daughter, when Our Divinity formed the Creation, It placed the Divine Will as raw material in all things, and so all things had their shape, solidity, order and beauty. And everything the soul does with this raw material of my Will, since a vital act flows within it, receives from It the shape of the beautiful works, all ordered and solid, with the imprint of the life of the Divine Fiat within each work. On the other hand, one who does not do my Will and does not put It as raw material in his works, might do perhaps many things, but all disordered, without shape, without beauty, all scattered, such that he himself would not know how to make head or tail of them. It would happen as if someone wanted to make bread without water; he might perhaps have much flour, but since the water is missing, the life to form the bread would be missing. Someone else might have many stones in order to build, but does not have the lime that unites and cements the stones together; so, he would have a disorder of stones, but never a house. Such are the works without the raw material of my Will; they only occupy space, they cause bother, annoyance; and if they do any good at all, it is superficial – if they are touched, they are found to be fragile and empty of any good."

Volume 25

October 10, 1928

Forty years and more of exile; virtue and strength of a prolonged sacrifice. Gathering of the materials, to then order them. Happiness of Jesus in blessing His little prisoner daughter. Kisses in the Divine Will. Decision from priests to prepare the writings for printing. Surprising graces that Jesus will give to priests.

My life is carried out before my Jesus in the Sacrament, and – oh! how many thoughts crowd my mind. I was thinking to myself: 'After forty years, and months, that I had not seen the Tabernacle, that I had not been given to be before His adorable sacramental presence – forty years, not only of prison, but of exile – finally, and after so long an exile, I have come back as though to my fatherland, though a prisoner, but no longer exiled, near my Jesus in the Sacrament; and not once a day, as I used to do before Jesus made me a prisoner, but always – always. My poor heart, if I have it at all in my chest, feels consumed at so much love of Jesus.' But while I was thinking of this and other things, my Highest Good, Jesus, moving in my interior, told me: "My daughter, do you think that my keeping you imprisoned for forty years and more has been by chance, without a great design of mine? No! no! The number forty has always been significant and preparatory to great works. For forty years the Jews walked in the desert without being able to reach the promised land, their fatherland; but after forty years of sacrifices they had the good of taking possession of it. But, how many miracles, how many graces, to the point of nourishing them with the celestial manna during that time. A prolonged sacrifice has the virtue and strength to obtain great things from God. I Myself, during my life down here, wanted to remain in the desert for forty days, away from all, even from my Mama, to then go out in public to announce the Gospel which was to form the life of my Church – that is, the Kingdom of Redemption. For forty days I wanted to remain as risen, to confirm my Resurrection and to place the seal upon all the goods of Redemption. So I wanted for you, my daughter: in order to manifest the Kingdom of my Divine Will, I wanted forty years of sacrifices. But, how many graces have I not given you! How many manifestations! I can say that in this great length of time I placed in you all the capital of the Kingdom of my Will, and everything that is necessary in order to make creatures comprehend it. So, your long imprisonment has been the continual weapon, always in the act of fighting with your very Creator, to have you manifest my Kingdom.

Now, you must know that everything I have manifested to your soul, the graces I have given you, the many truths you have written on my Divine Will, your pains, and everything you have done, has been nothing but a gathering of the materials in order to build; and now it is necessary to order them and to get everything settled. And just as I did not leave you alone in gathering the necessary things which must serve my Kingdom, but I have been always with you, so will I not leave you alone in putting them in order and in showing the great building which I have been preparing together with you for many years. Therefore, our sacrifice and work is not finished. We must go forward until the work is accomplished."

Then, as I am near my Jesus in the Sacrament, every morning there is benediction with the Most Holy One, and while I was praying my sweet Jesus to bless me, moving in my interior, He told me: "My daughter, I bless you with my whole Heart; even more, I bless my very Will in you, I bless your thoughts, breaths and heartbeats, that you may think always about my Will, may breath It continuously, and my Will alone may be your heartbeat. And for love of you I bless all human wills, that they may dispose themselves to receive the Life of my Eternal Volition. Dearest daughter of mine, if you knew how sweet it is, how happy I feel in blessing the little daughter of my Will…. My Heart rejoices in blessing she who possesses the origin, the Life of Our Fiat, which will bring about the beginning, the origin of the Kingdom of my Divine Will. And while I bless you, I pour in you the beneficial dew of the light of my Divine Volition which, making you all shining, will make you appear more beautiful to my sacramental gazes; and I will feel happier in this cell, gazing at my little prisoner daughter, invested and bound by the sweet chains of my Will. And every time I bless you, I will make the Life of my Divine Volition grow in you. How beautiful is the company of one who does my Divine Will. My Will brings into the depth of the soul the echo of everything I do in this Holy Host, and I do not feel alone in my acts – I feel that she is praying together with Me; and as our supplications, our sighs, unite together, we ask for one same thing – that the Divine Will be known and that Its Kingdom come soon."

So, as my life is carried out near my Prisoner Jesus, every time the door of the chapel is opened, which happens often, I send three kisses, or five, to my Jesus in the Sacrament, or a short little visit; and He, moving in my interior, tells me: "My daughter, how pleasing to Me are your kisses. I feel I am being kissed by you with the kisses of my very Volition; I feel my very divine kisses being impressed on my lips, on my face, in my hands and Heart. Everything is divine in the soul in whom my Divine Will reigns; and I feel, in your acts, my love that refreshes Me, the freshness, the gentleness of my very Divine Will that embraces Me, kisses Me and loves Me. Oh! how pleasing to Me is my Divine Will operating in the creature. I feel that, bilocating Me in her, It gives Me back and unfolds before Me all the beauty and sanctity of my very acts. This is why I so much yearn that my Will be known – to be able to find in creatures all of my acts, divine and worthy of Me."

Now I move on to say that my sweet Jesus seemed to be waiting for me here, in this House, near His Tabernacle of love, to give start to priests' coming to a decision to prepare the writings for publication. And while they were consulting with one another on how to do it, they were reading the nine excesses of Jesus, which He had in the Incarnation, which are narrated in the first little volume of my writings. Now, while they were reading, Jesus, in my interior, pricked up His ears to listen, and it seemed to me that Jesus in the Tabernacle would do the same. At each word He would hear, His Heart beat more strongly; and at each excess of His love, He gave a start, even stronger, as if the strength of His love would make Him repeat all those excesses which He had in the Incarnation. And as though unable to contain His flames, He told me: "My daughter, everything I have told you, both about my Incarnation and about my Divine Will, and on other things, has been nothing but outpourings of my contained love. But after pouring itself out with you, my love continued to remain repressed, because it wanted to raise its flames higher in order to invest all hearts and make known what I have done and want to do for creatures; but since everything I have told you lies in hiddenness, I feel a nightmare over my Heart, which compresses Me and prevents my flames from rising and making their way. This is why, as I heard them read and take the decision to occupy themselves with the publication, I felt the nightmare being removed from Me, and the weight that compresses the flames of my Heart being lifted. And so It beat more strongly, and It throbbed, and It made you hear the repetition of all those excesses of love; more so, since what I do once, I repeat always. My constrained love is a pain for Me, of the greatest, which renders Me taciturn and sad, because, since my first flames have no life, I cannot release the others, which devour Me and consume Me. And therefore, to those priests who want to occupy themselves with removing this nightmare from Me by making known my many secrets, by publishing them, I will give so much surprising grace, strength in order to do it, and light in order to know, themselves first, what they will make known to others. I will be in their midst, and will guide everything."

Now, it seems to me that every time the Reverend priests occupy themselves with reviewing the writings in order to prepare them, my sweet Jesus comes to attention, to see what they do and how they do it. I do nothing but admire the goodness, the love of my beloved Jesus who, while coming to attention in my Heart, echoes in the Tabernacle, and from within it, inside that cell, does what He does inside my heart. I remain all confused in seeing this, and I thank Him with all my heart.

Volume 25

December 16, 1928

Speaking of the nine excesses of Jesus in the Incarnation. Contentments of Jesus. His word is creation. Jesus sees the scenes of His love being repeated. Preludes of His Kingdom.

I was doing my meditation, and since today it was the beginning of the Novena of Baby Jesus, I was thinking about the nine excesses of His Incarnation, which Jesus had narrated to me with so much tenderness, and which are written in the first volume. I felt great reluctance at reminding the confessor about this, because, in reading them, he had told me that he wanted to read them in public in our chapel.

Now, while I was thinking of this, my little Baby Jesus made Himself seen in my arms, so very little, caressing me with His tiny little hands, and saying to me: "How beautiful is my little daughter! How beautiful! How I must thank you for having listened to Me." And I: 'My Love, what are You saying? It is I who must thank You for having spoken to me, and for having given me, with so much love, acting as my teacher, so many lessons which I did not deserve.' And Jesus: "Ah, my daughter, to how many do I want to speak, and they do not listen to Me, reducing Me to silence and to suffocating my flames. So, we must thank each other – you thank Me, and I thank you. And then, why do you want to oppose the reading of the nine excesses? Ah! You do not know how much life, how much love and grace they contain. You must know that my word is creation, and in narrating to you the nine excesses of my love in the Incarnation, I not only renewed my love which I had in incarnating Myself, but I created new love in order to invest the creatures and conquer them to give themselves to Me. These nine excesses of my love, manifested with so much love of tenderness and simplicity, formed the prelude of the many lessons I was to give you about my Divine Fiat, in order to form Its Kingdom. And now, by their being read, my love is renewed and redoubled. Don't you want, then, that my love, being redoubled, overflow outside and invest more hearts, so that, as a prelude, they may dispose themselves for the lessons of my Will, to make It known and reign?" And I: 'My dear Baby, I believe that many have spoken about your Incarnation.' And Jesus: "Yes, yes, they have spoken, but those have been words taken from the shore of my love, therefore they are words which possess neither tendernesses, nor fulnesses of life. But those few words which

I have spoken to you, I have spoken from within the life of the fount of my love, and they contain life, irresistible strength, and such tendernesses, that only the dead will not feel themselves being moved to pity for Me, tiny little One, who suffered so many pains even from the womb of the Celestial Mama."

After this, the confessor was reading in the chapel the first excess of the love of Jesus in the Incarnation; and my sweet Jesus, from within my interior, pricked up His ears to listen. And drawing me to Himself, He said to me: "My daughter, how happy I feel in listening to them. But my happiness increases in keeping you in this house of my Will, as both of us are listeners: I, of what I have told you, and you, of what you have heard from Me. My love swells, boils and overflows. Listen, listen – how beautiful it is! The word contains the breath, and as it is spoken, the word carries the breath which, like air, goes around from mouth to mouth and communicates the strength of my creative word; and the new creation which my word contains descends into the hearts. Listen, my daughter: in Redemption I had the cortege of my Apostles, and I was in their midst, all love, in order to instruct them; I spared no toil in order to form the foundation of my Church. Now, in this house, I feel the cortege of the first children of my Will, and I feel my loving scenes being repeated, in seeing you in their midst, all love, wanting to impart the lessons about my Divine Fiat in order to form the foundations of the Kingdom of my Divine Will. If you knew how happy I feel in seeing you speak about my Divine Volition…. I anxiously await the moment when you begin to speak, in order to listen to you, and to feel the happiness that my Divine Will brings Me".

Volume 25

December 21, 1928

Sea of love in the excesses of Jesus. Example of the sea. The Divine Will, solar ray which brings the Life of Heaven. The Divine Will operating. Happiness of Jesus.

The novena of Holy Christmas continues, and continuing to hear the nine excesses of the Incarnation, my beloved Jesus drew me to Himself, and showed me how each excess of His love was a sea without boundaries. And, in this sea, gigantic waves rose, in which one could see all souls flowing, devoured by these flames. Just as the fish flow in the waters of the sea, and the waters of the sea form the life of the fish, the guide, the defense, the food, the bed, the palace of these fish, so much so, that if they get out of the sea, they can say, "our life is ended, because we have gone out of our inheritance – the fatherland given to us by our Creator"; in the same way, these gigantic waves of flames which rose from these seas of fire, by devouring the creatures, wanted to be the life, the guide, the defense, the food, the bed, the palace, the fatherland of creatures. But as they go out of this sea of love, all of a sudden, they find death. And little Baby Jesus cries, moans, prays, shouts and sighs, for He wants no one to go out of these devouring flames of His, because He does not want to see anyone die. Oh! if the sea had reason, more than tender mother it would sadly cry over its fish which are snatched away from its sea, because it feels a life, which it possesses and preserves with so much love, being snatched away from itself; and with its waves, it would hurl itself at those who dared to snatch away from it so many lives which it possesses, and which form its richness, its glory.

"And if the sea does not cry, I cry" – Jesus says – "in seeing that, while my love has devoured all creatures, ungrateful, they do not want to live life in my sea of love, but wriggling free from my flames, they exile themselves from my Fatherland, losing the palace, the guide, the defense, the food, the bed, and even the life. How can I not cry? They came out of Me – they were created by Me, and were devoured by my flames of love which I had in incarnating Myself for love of all creatures. As I hear the nine excesses being narrated to Me, the sea of my love swells – it boils; and forming huge waves, it roars so much, that it would want to deafen everyone, that they might hear nothing but my moans of love, my cries of sorrow, my repeated sobs, saying: 'Don't make Me cry any more, let us exchange the kiss of peace; let us love each other, and we will all be happy – the Creator and the creature'."

Jesus kept silent, and at that moment I saw the heavens opened and a ray of light descend from above, which, fixing itself upon me, illuminated those who were around me. And my always lovable Jesus resumed His speaking: "Daughter of my Will, this solar ray that fixed itself upon you is my Divine Will, which brings you the life of Heaven into your soul. How beautiful is this solar ray, which not only illuminates you and brings you its life, but whoever draws near you and remains around feels the life of light, because, like sun, it expands around, and gives to those who surround you the warm kiss of light, of its breath, of its life. And I feel happy within you in seeing that my Divine Will diffuses and begins to beat its way. See, the seas of love that you saw are nothing other than my Will operating. When my Will wants to operate, the seas of my love swell, boil, form their gigantic waves which cry, moan, shout, pray, deafen. On the other hand, when my Fiat does not want to operate, the sea of my love is calm, it only murmurs quietly, its course of joy and of happiness, inseparable from it, is continuous. Therefore, you cannot comprehend the joy I experience, the happiness I feel and the interest I take in illuminating, in offering my very word, my very Heart, to one who occupies himself with making my Divine Will known. My interest is so great, that I envelop him within Myself and, I Myself overflowing outside of him, I take the floor, and I Myself speak about my Will operating in my love. Do you think that it is your confessor that speaks, in these evenings in which he is speaking in public about the nine excesses of my love? It is I who take his heart in my hands and make him speak."

But while He was saying this, benediction was being given, and Jesus added: "Daughter, I bless you; everything is happiness for Me when it comes to doing an act of mine over one who possesses my Divine Will, because, if I bless you, my blessing finds the space in which to place the goods and the effects which my blessing contains; if I love you, my love finds in my Fiat, within you, the space in which to place itself and carry out its life of love. Therefore, each thing I do over you, in you and with you, is a happiness that I feel, because I know that a Divine Will has the place for everything I want to give you, and the virtue of multiplying the goods I give you, because It is Our all-doer, and It occupies Itself with forming as many lives for as many acts as We do with the creature in whom It reigns."

After this, I was doing my round in the Divine Fiat, and was going again to the first times of Creation, to unite myself to the acts done by our father Adam in the state of innocence, so as to unite myself with him and continue from where he left. And my beloved Jesus, moving in my interior, told me: "My daughter, in creating man I gave a visible universe in which he was to move freely and see the works of his Creator, done with so much order and harmony, done for love of him, and, in this void, to also do his own works. And just as I gave a visible void, so I gave an invisible void, even more beautiful, for his soul, in which man was to form his holy works, his sun, his heavens, his stars; and echoing his Creator, he was to fill this void with all his works. But since man descended from my Divine Will to live in his own, he lost the echo of his Creator and the model with which to be able to copy Our works. Therefore, it can be said that in this void there is nothing other than the first steps of man – all the rest is empty. Yet, it must be filled, and this is why I await with so much love those who live and must live in my Will, who, feeling the power of our echo and having Our models present to them, will hasten to fill this invisible void which I gave with so much love in Creation. But do you know what this void is? It is Our Will. Just as I gave a heaven, a sun, to man's nature, so I gave the Heaven, the Sun of my Fiat to his soul. And when I see you take your steps after the steps of Adam innocent, I say: 'Finally, here is the void of my Divine Will that begins to receive the first conquests and the first works of the creature.' Therefore, be attentive and continue always your flight in my Divine Volition."

Volume 25

December 25, 1928

The feast which the little daughter prepares for Baby Jesus; how she renders Him happy. Adam, first sun. Example of the artisan.

I was thinking about the birth of Baby Jesus, and I prayed Him to come to be born in my poor soul. And in order to sing His praises and form a cortege for Him in the act of His birth, I fused myself in the Holy Divine Volition, and flowing in all created things, I wanted to animate the heavens, the sun, the stars, the sea, the earth and everything with my *'I love You'*. I wanted to place all created things as though in waiting, in the act of Jesus' birth, so that all would say to Him *'I love You'* and *'we want the Kingdom of your Will upon earth'*.

Now, while I was doing this, it seemed to me that all created things would come to attention in the act of Jesus' birth, and as the dear Baby came out of the womb of His Celestial Mama, the heavens, the sun, and even the tiny little bird, as though all in chorus, were saying, *'I love You'* and *'we want the Kingdom of your Will upon earth'*. My *'I love You'* in the Divine Will flowed within all things in which the Divine Will had Its life, and therefore all sang praises to the birth of their Creator; and I saw the newborn Baby who, flinging Himself into my arms, all shivering, told me: "What a beautiful feast has the little daughter of my Will prepared for Me; how beautiful is the chorus of all created things saying to Me *'I love You'*, and wanting my Will to reign. One who lives in It can give Me anything, and can use all stratagems in order to render Me happy and make Me smile, even in the midst of tears. Therefore, I was waiting for you, to have a surprise of love of yours by virtue of my Divine Volition. In fact, you must know that my life on earth was nothing but suffering, operating and preparing everything that was to serve the Kingdom of my Divine Will, which must be Kingdom of happiness and of possession; therefore, it is then that my works will have their full fruits and will change for Me and for creatures into sweetnesses, into joys and into possession."

Now, while He was saying this, He disappeared from me; but after a little while He came back, inside a little cradle of gold, clothed with a tiny little garment of light. And He added: "My daughter, today is my birthday, and I have come to render you happy with my presence. It would be too hard for Me, on this day, not to render one who lives in my Divine Will happy, not to give you my first kiss and tell you *'I love you'* as a requital of yours, and, clasping you tightly to my little Heart, make you feel my heartbeats that unleash fire, and would want to burn everything which does not belong to my Will, while your heartbeat, echoing within mine, repeats for Me your pleasant refrain: *'May your Will reign on earth as It does in Heaven'*. Repeat it always, if you want to render Me happy and calm my baby crying. Look – your love has prepared for Me the gold cradle, and the acts in my Divine Will have prepared for Me the little garment of light. Aren't you happy?"

After this, I continued my acts in the Divine Fiat, going back to Eden, into the first acts of the creation of man; and my sweet Jesus, moving in my interior, told me: "My daughter, Adam was the first human sun, invested by Our Volition, and his acts were more than sun's rays which, extending and expanding, were to invest the whole human family, in which one would see many in one, as though palpitating in these rays, all centralized in the center of this first human sun. And all were to have the virtue of forming their own suns, without going out of the bond of the first sun. In fact, since the life of each one would have its origin from this sun, each one would be able to be sun of his own. How beautiful was the creation of man. O! how it surpassed the whole entire universe. The bond, the union of one in many, was the greatest prodigy of Our Omnipotence, as Our Will, one in Itself, was to maintain the inseparability of all, the communicative and unifying life of all – symbol and image of Our Divinity, as We are inseparable, and even though We are three Divine Persons, We are always one, because one is the Will, one is the sanctity, one is Our power. This is why man is always looked upon by Us as if there were one alone, even though he was to have his very long generation, but always centralized in the one. It was the uncreated love that was created by Us in man, and therefore he was to give of Us and be like Us; and Our Will, the only one acting in Us, was to act as the only one in man, in order to form the unity of all and the bond of inseparability of each one.

Therefore, by withdrawing from Our Divine Fiat, man became deformed and disordered, and no longer felt the strength of the unity and inseparability, either with his Creator or with all generations. He felt like a divided body, broken in his members, which no longer possesses all the strength of his body as whole. This is why my Divine Will wants to enter again as prime act into the creature – to reunite the broken members and to give him the unity and the inseparability, as he came out of Our creative hands. We find Ourselves in the condition of an artisan who has made his beautiful statue, such as to astonish Heaven and earth. The artisan loves this statue so much that he has placed his very life in it; so, at each act or movement it does, the artisan feels within himself the life, the act, the movement of his beautiful statue. The artisan loves it with love of delirium, nor can he remove his gaze from it; but in so much love, the statue receives an encounter, it bumps, and it remains broken in its members and in its vital part which kept it bound and united to the artisan. What will his sorrow not be? And what will he not do in order to redo his beautiful statue? More so, since he still loves it, and to the raving love has added the grieving love. Such is the state the Divinity is in with regard to man. He is Our delirium of love and of sorrow, for We want to redo the beautiful statue of man; and since the bump took place in the vital part of Our Will which he possessed, once Our Will is reestablished in him, the beautiful statue will be redone for Us, and Our love will be satisfied. Therefore, I want nothing else from you but my Divine Will to have Its life." Then He added with a more tender tone: "My daughter, in the created things the Divinity did not create love, but the flowerings of His light, of His power, of His beauty, etc. So, it can be said that in creating the heavens, the stars, the sun, the wind, the sea, the earth, it was Our works that We issued, and the flowerings of Our beautiful qualities. Only for man was this greatest prodigy of creating the life – and the life of Our love itself; and this is why it is said that he was created in Our image and likeness. And this is why We love him so much – because it is life and work that has come out of Us, and life costs more than anything."

Volume 27

December 25, 1929

How the birth of Jesus was the rebirth of the Divine Will in His Humanity, and everything He did were rebirths of It, formed in Him in order to make It be reborn in creatures. Jesus was the true Sacrificed One of His Will.

I was thinking of when my most sweet Baby Jesus, fidgeting with love, came out of the womb of His Celestial Mama. What joy for Her to be able to squeeze Him in Her arms, kiss Him, and engage in a contest in loving the One who so much loved Her. But while many thoughts were crowding my mind about the holy birth of the Divine Infant, I felt Him move in my interior, and coming outside, He placed Himself in my arms, and stretching out His tiny little hands to my neck, He told me: "My daughter, you too – kiss Me and squeeze Me to yourself, as I kiss you and squeeze you to Myself; and let us love each other with such contest of love as to never stop." And abandoning Himself in my arms as a tiny little Baby, He remained silent. But who can say the squeezes of love, the affectionate kisses? I believe it is better to pass over them in silence.

Then, afterwards, resuming His speaking, He added: "My daughter, my birth in time was the rebirth of my Divine Will in my Humanity; and as It was reborn in Me, It brought the good news of Its rebirth in the human generations. My Fiat is eternal, but it can be said that It was as though born in Adam in order to form the long generation of the rebirth in the creature. But since Adam rejected this Divine Will, by rejecting It, he prevented the many rebirths It was to have in each creature; and with constant and invincible love It waited for my Humanity in order to be born again in the midst of the human family. Therefore, everything I did in the whole course of my Life – the baby tears, my moans and wailings – were nothing other than rebirths of my Divine Will that were formed in Me so as to make It be reborn in creatures. In fact, It being reborn in Me, and possessing It as my own, I had the right and the power to give It and make It be reborn in the creature. So, everything that my Humanity would do – steps, works, words, pains, and even my breath, and my very death – formed as many rebirths of my Divine Will for as many creatures as would have the good of the rebirth of my Divine Fiat. Since I am the head of the human family, and it, my members, as the head I called with my acts – I called the many rebirths of my Divine Volition within Me, to let them pass to be reborn in my members, the creatures.

Therefore, there was not one act I did – even my very Sacramental Life, each consecrated Host, are continuous rebirths of my Supreme Volition, which It prepares for the creature. So, I am the true Sacrificed One of a cause so holy – that my Will may reign. I Myself am the One who formed Its Kingdom within Me; and making It be reborn in Me as many times for as many creatures as It would be reborn in, I formed Its most holy empire and Its reigning in the midst of my members.

Now, my daughter, after I placed the Kingdom of my Divine Will in safety within my Humanity, I had to manifest It in order to make It known. Therefore I came to you and I began to narrate to you the long story of my Divine Fiat. Now, you must know that I have made and I make so many manifestations, I have spoken so many truths, so many words, for as many rebirths as my Will did in my Humanity. Its rebirths in Me and Its knowledges that I manifest to you will be in perfect balance; each rebirth of my Divine Volition done in Me and in each consecrated Host will find a manifestation and a truth of Its own that confirms It, and will give It rebirth in the creature. In fact, in God the word forms the life of the good He wants to form in the creature; Our word is bearer of life. Was is not Our word *'Fiat'* that, pronouncing Itself, created the heavens, the sun and everything that can be seen in the entire universe, and even the very life of man himself? Until We pronounced *'Fiat'*, everything was in Us; as It was pronounced, It populated heavens and earth with so many works, beautiful and worthy of Us, and It gave the start to the long generation of so many human lives. See, then, how everything I tell you on my Divine Will will bring, with the power of my creative word, Its many rebirths done in Me into the midst of the human family. Here is the great reason for a story so long and a speaking of mine so continuous. It will be in balance with everything that was done by Us in Creation, and with everything I did in Redemption. And if it seems that sometimes I remain silent, it is not because I have ceased my speaking, but because I take rest. In fact, it is my usual way to rest in my very word and works that come out of Me. Just as I did in Creation – It was not pronounced always; I would say *'Fiat'* and I would pause, and then I would pronounce It again – so I do in you: I speak, I give you my lesson and I take rest; first, to enjoy in you the effects of my words; and to dispose you to receive the new life of my lesson. Therefore, be attentive, and let your flight in my Divine Will be continuous."

Volume 35

December 25, 1937

The descent of the Divine Word. How He left Heaven, while still remaining there. Prodigies of the Incarnation. The beginning of the feast of the Divine Will. How in His Divine works He puts aside human ingratitude. The grafting. How the Love of Jesus

I was following the acts of the Divine Volition, and my poor mind paused in the act of the descent of the Divine Word upon earth. My God! How many wonders, how many surprises of Love, of Power, of Divine Wisdom! They are so great and so many that one doesn't know where to start to tell them.

My beloved Jesus, as if inundated in His sea of Love which forms Its waves, surprising me said: "My blessed daughter, in my descent upon earth the wonders – the ardor of our Love – were so great and so many that neither Angels nor creatures can understand all that our Divinity operated in the mystery of my Incarnation. You must know that our Supreme Being possesses Its incessant motion by nature. If this motion could cease, even for an instant – which cannot be – all things would remain paralyzed and with no life, because all things – the life, the preservation and all that exists in Heaven and on earth – everything – depends on that Motion. Therefore, in descending from Heaven to earth, I, Word and Son of the Father, departed from our primary Motion; I mean – remaining, I left. The Father and the Holy Spirit descended with Me – they were concurrent (neither did I do any act if not together with Them), and they still remained on the Throne – full of Majesty, in the Celestial regions.

So, as I left, my Immensity, my Love and my Power descended together with Me; and my Love – which is incredible and is not satisfied if It doesn't form, from my Life, a Life for each existing creature – not only did this, but It formed my Life everywhere and in every place – multiplying It. Keeping my Immensity in Its power, My Love filled It with many of my Lives, so that everyone could have a Life of mine for himself, and the Divinity could have the glory and the honor of a Divine Life for as many things and creatures as We delivered to daylight. Ah! our Love repaid Us for the Work of Creation. And by forming many of our Lives, It not only repaid Us, but It gave Us even more than We had done. Our Divinity remained enraptured, and felt a sweet enchantment in seeing the devices and stratagems of our Love – in seeing so many of our Lives being spread out, since our Love used our own Immensity as the circle in which to place them. Therefore, while my Life was the center, my Immensity and Power were the circumference in which these innumerable Lives were being deposited. These Lives could find everything and everyone, and offered themselves to love Us and to be loved."

I remained surprised in hearing this, and my sweet Jesus, not giving me time, immediately added: "My daughter, don't be surprised. When We operate, We do complete works, so that nobody can ever say: 'He didn't do this for me. His Life is not all my own.' Ah, love cannot arise when things are not one's own and are not kept within one's power. And then, isn't this what the Sun also does – work created by Us – in becoming light for the eyes, to the extent of filling them completely with light, and being, at the same time, light – full and entire – for the hand that works, for the step that walks…? In this way, everyone – created things and creatures – can say: 'The Sun is mine.' While the center of the Sun is in the height of the atmosphere, its light departs and remains. With its circle of light it invests the earth and becomes light for everyone – even for the little flower and the tiny blade of grass.

The Sun is not life. It has light, and light it gives, together with all the goods contained in its light. Our Divinity is Life – the Author and Life of all. Therefore, in descending from Heaven to earth I had to do complete acts, and – more than Sun – show off my Life, multiplying it into many Lives, so that Heaven, earth and everyone could possess my Life. Otherwise, it would not have been a work worthy of our Wisdom and of our infinite Love."

Jesus remained silent, and I continued to think about the birth of Little Baby Jesus. And He added: "Little daughter of my Will, the feast of my birth was the feast – the beginning of the feast – of my Divine Will. As the Angels were singing, 'Glory to God in the highest Heavens, and peace on earth to the men of good will,' all Angels and the Creation assumed a festive mode and, while celebrating my birth, they celebrated the feast of my Divine Will. In fact, with my birth, our Divinity received true glory unto the highest Heavens; and men will have the true peace, when they will recognize my Will, giving It dominion and allowing It to reign. Only then, they will feel my Will as good – will they feel the divine strength; only then, will Heaven and earth sing together: 'Glory to God in the highest Heavens, and peace on earth to the men who will possess the Divine Will.' All will abound in these men, and they will possess the true peace."

So, I continued to think of the birth of the little King Jesus, and I said to Him: 'Nice Little Baby, tell me, what did you do when you saw the great human ingratitude to your great Love?' And Jesus: "My daughter, if I had taken into account the human ingratitude to my great Love, I would have taken the way to go back to Heaven; but I would have saddened and embittered my Love, and turned the feast into mourning. So, would you like to know what I do in my greatest works in order to make them more beautiful? With pomp and with the greatest show of my Love, I put everything aside – human ingratitude, sins, miseries, weaknesses – and I give course to my greatest works, as if those things did not exist. If I had wanted to care about the evils of man, I couldn't have done great works, or put all my Love on the field. I would have remain hampered – suffocated in my own Love. Instead, in order to be free in my works, and to make them as beautiful as I can, I place everything aside and, if necessary, I cover everything with my Love, so that I see nothing but my Love and my Will. I move forward with my greatest works, and I perform them as if nobody had offended Me. For Our Glory, nothing can be lacking to Our decorum – to the beauty and the greatness of Our works.

This is why I would want that you too did not occupy yourselves with your weaknesses, your evils and your troubles. In fact, the more the creature thinks about those, the weaker she feels, and the more the poor one feels drowned by evils, while her miseries press round her more strongly. By thinking about it, weakness feeds more weakness, and the poor creature falls even more; evils become stronger, miseries reduce her to starvation. But if she doesn't think about them, they disappear by themselves.

Good is completely the opposite. One good feeds another good – one act of love calls for more love. One abandonment in my Will makes her feel the new Divine Life within herself. Therefore, thinking of good, forms the food and the strength to do more good. This is why I want your thinking to be occupied by nothing other than loving me and living in my Will. My Love will burn all your miseries and all your evils, and my Divine Volition will become your Life, using your miseries as the base on which to raise Its Throne."

Then, I continued to think about the little newborn Jesus – and oh, how it broke my heart seeing him crying, sobbing, wailing and shivering with cold! I wanted to place one I love you of mine for each pain and each tear of the Divine Little One, to warm him and to calm his crying. And Jesus added: "My daughter, I can feel one who lives in my Will in my tears and in my wailing. I feel her flowing in my crying sobs and in the shivering of my tiny limbs. By virtue of my Will which she possesses, she turns the tears into smiles, and the sobs into Heavenly joys. With her love dirges, she warms me and changes the pains into kisses and hugs. Even more, know that one who lives in my Will receives continuous grafts of all that my Humanity does. If I think, I graft her thoughts; if I speak and pray, I graft her word; if I work, I graft her hands – there is nothing of what I do that does not form a graft for the creature, to make of her the repetition of my Life; even more so, since my Divine Will is in her, and I can find my Power, my Sanctity and my very Life, to do whatever I want with her.

How many prodigies can I not do, when I find my Will in the creature? I came on earth to cover everything with my Love, to drown the very evils, and to burn everything with my Love. By justice, I wanted to repay my Father, because it was right for Him to be restored in His honor, in the glory, in the love and in the gratitude that everyone owed Him – so, my Love couldn't find peace. It fills the gaps of His glory and of His honor; to the extent that, through love, It repaid the Divinity Who had created a Heaven, a Sun, a wind, a sea, a flowery earth, and all the rest, while man had uttered not even one 'Thank you', for the so many goods he had received. He had been the true thief – the ungrateful – the usurper of our goods. My Love ran and ran in order to fill the abysses of distance between the Creator and the creature. It paid my Celestial Father through love, and through love It bought back the human generations, to give back to them the Life of my Divine Will, having already formed many Lives from It, as their ransom. And when my Love pays, the value is such that It can afford to pay for everyone, and to buy back whatever It wants. Therefore, you have already been purchased by my Love; so, let me enjoy you, and possess you."

FIAT!!!

Volume 36

December 25, 1938

The descent of the Word. How easy it is to make Jesus be born as long as we live in His Will. The Paradise that the Queen of Heaven made Jesus find on earth.

My poor mind continues its path in the Divine Will. O! how happy It feels in seeing that Its little newborn wanders in search of its acts, to know them, kiss them, adore them, make them her own, and say: 'how much You loved me.' I stopped at the descent of the Word upon earth, and I felt sorry in seeing Him all alone. My sweet Jesus, with unspeakable tenderness, surprising me, told me: "My dearest daughter, you're wrong. Loneliness is part of human ingratitude; but from the divine side, all our works accompanied me, never leaving me alone. Further, you must know that the Father and the Holy Spirit descended together with me, while I still remained in Heaven with them. They came down on earth within me, since we are inseparable. We cannot be separated, not even if we wished to be so – at the most we bilocate ourselves, so as to maintain our Throne in Heaven while forming our throne on earth. Being separated – never. At the most, the Word took the operative part, but always with the concourse of the Father and the Holy Spirit.

Furthermore, in the act of my descent from Heaven, everyone moved to be my court and render me the honors I deserve. The Sky courted me with all its stars, rendering me the honor of my immutability and of my everlasting love. The Sun courted me, paying me the honor of my eternal light – oh! how well it praised the variety of its effects. I can say that, as I found myself with its light and heat, in its mute language it told me: 'You are the light, and I honor you, I adore you, I love you with the same light with which you created me.' All surrounded me: the wind, the sea, the little bird – everyone and everything, to give me the love and the glory with which I had created them. And they praised my empire, my immensity, my infinite joys. All created things made me a feast, and if I cried they cried together with me, because my Will, residing in them, kept them aware of all that I was doing. O!, how honored they felt, in doing all that their Creator was doing. Then I received the courting of the Angels, who never left me alone. And since all times belong to me, I was also courted by all the many peoples, who were going to live in my Will. My Will was carrying them in Its arms, and I felt them beating in my Heart, in my blood and in my steps. In feeling invested by these people, loved by my own Will, I felt repaid for my descent from Heaven to earth.

This was my primary scope: to reorder the Kingdom of my Will in the midst of my children. I would never have created the world if I was not to have children who looked like me and lived in my own Will. My Will would find Itself in the same condition as a poor sterile mother who is not able to generate, and therefore form her own family. But my Will does have the power to generate and to form Its long generations – Its own family." Then I continued to think about the descent of the

Divine Word, saying to myself: how could Jesus be born within our souls? And my Dear Baby said: "My daughter, to make me be born is the easiest thing – more so, since we do not know how to do difficult things. Our power facilitates everything. Provided that the creature lives in our Will, all is done. As soon as the soul wants to live in It, she has already formed the home for your Jesus; at the moment she wants to start doing her acts, she conceives me; as she does her act, she makes me be born. As she loves in my Will, so she clothes me with light, warming me from the great coldness of the creatures. Every time she gives me her will to take my own, I am amused – I have my toy to play with, and I sing my victory over the human will, feeling like the little Triumphant King.

See then, my daughter, how easy this is for your little Jesus, because when we find our Will in the creature, we can do anything. It provides us with all that is needed and all that we want, to form our Life and our most beautiful works. But without our Will, we remain hampered: now love is missing, now sanctity, now power, now purity, and all that it takes to make our Life rise again and to form it within the creatures. Therefore, all depends on the creatures, since, from our side, we place ourselves at their disposal.

Further, during my birth my Divine Mama made me a beautiful surprise with her acts, with her love – with the Life of my Will which she possessed. She formed my Paradise on earth. She did nothing other than braid the whole Creation with her love, laying seas of beauty – making me enjoy our divine beauties within which her beauty was shining. How beautiful my Mother was – how beautiful to find her in the whole of Creation; she made me enjoy her beauty and the beauty of her acts. She spread her sea of love to make me find her love – my Paradise of love – in all created things. I delighted and exulted in my Mama's seas of love. She made for me, in my

Will, the most beautiful tunes and the most delightful concerts, so that her little Jesus would not miss the music of the Heavenly Fatherland. My Mother took care of everything, so that nothing would be lacking of the enjoyment of the Paradise I had left. She kept forming, in each one of her acts, new joys to make me happy. By just leaning on her Heart I could feel such harmonies and contents as to be enraptured. By living in my Will, my Dear Mother carried Paradise in her lap and let her Son enjoy it. All her acts did nothing less than make me happy and redouble my Paradise on earth.

Now, my daughter, let me tell you another surprise. One who lives in my Will is inseparable from me; she is born again each time together with me. Therefore, I am never alone. I make her be born again with me to divine life – to new love, to new sanctity and to new beauty. She is reborn in the knowledge of her Creator – reborn in each one of her acts. More than this, in every act she does, she calls me to be born again, forming a new Paradise for her Jesus; and I make her be born again with me, to make her happy. One of my greatest joys is to make those who live together with me happy. Therefore, be attentive to live in my Will if you want to make me happy – if you want me to find in your acts my Paradise on earth; and I will take care to make you enjoy the sea of my joy and happiness. We will make each other happy."

FIAT!!!!!

LUISA'S LETTERS

In Voluntate Dei!

16. My good and Reverend Mother General,

thank you for your wishes; I return them to you from the heart. Forgive me if I delayed in answering you, as it was convenient for me to play with my Little Baby Jesus, and then to think of my duty of answering Your Maternity. And you know that many times one loses the game and remains upset, and tries to repeat the game in order to win; therefore it takes time and patience (I am joking).

Now, my most dear Mother, I send you my best wishes: Christmas has gone, Jesus is born, and as my wishes, I send you little Jesus shivering with cold, His face wet with graceful tears, carrying His present in His little hands. But do you know what that is? His Divine Fiat. What a beautiful present He wants to give you! The gift is great, but He doesn't want to be with nothing in His little hands. My Mother, He is little, and wants to hold something to play with; He wants your will as gift, so He will find something to amuse Himself with. Aren't you happy? Therefore, my wish is great: I send you a most delicate task – to make the little Infant not be born, but grow with your love, to calm His crying and make Him smile by telling Him that you gladly accept the present of His Will, giving Him yours. In sum, you will make Him grow so much that you yourself will become the veil that covers Jesus.

My Mother, it is true that my wishes come from a little ignorant one, but you must know that it is the delirium, the fever, that devours me, as I yearn that the Divine Will reign in the hearts, and that we be the repeaters of the life of the Little Baby.

Now I pass on to send my wishes to the whole community and to the little orphans, by sending the greetings, the kiss, the present which Baby Jesus wants to give to all of them. And I beg all of them not to send Him back, otherwise they will make Him cry; and then how much will it take to soothe His tears.

In a special way I send my most heartfelt wishes to my good Mother Nazarena; tell her that I always remember her, I will never forget her, and I wish that dear little Jesus will keep her company, and make her a saint – a great saint; and to pray for me.

I finish here, because dear Little Baby is in a hurry to come to you, to give you His present and receive yours. So I leave you in the place of honor of the Divine Will, in which Jesus wants you. I kiss your right hand with sincere respect, and I ask you to bless me.

The little daughter of the Divine Will

21. To Sister Remigia

Fiat – In Voluntate Dei!

My good daughter in the Divine Volition,

Thank you for your wishes, and from the heart I return them to you, just on this Christmas evening as I am writing you. The Celestial Baby is born; even more, since He is born in every instant. In every good act we do, every time we abandon ourselves in His arms, and every time we cry out from the depths of our heart: "Lord, I want to do your Will", the dear Little One repeats His birth. So, I won't wish you His birth, since He is born; but rather, to make Him grow, to love Him and then to warm Him, because He is shivering with cold, and His little lips are livid, so freezing is the air. He wants your ardent kisses, the air of your love to warm Him; His limbs are numb, and He wants your works, your movements done for love of Him, as clothes to be covered with; and as food He wants His Will reigning in you.

So, this is my wish: that you raise me the Divine Infant and make Him happy; and that you give your will into His little hands to play with, so that, after all the tears He sheds, He may find you to make Him smile. And then, the dear Little One wants to entrust you with another task: that you make all the girls around you know that they each possess Jesus in their hearts, and you must teach them how to make Him grow. If you do this, you can be tranquil, because you will form many tabernacles for little Jesus. However, I do not want, nor does Jesus want, that you lose peace. Look for the Divine Will in everything, and your being will become continuous prayer, in everything. It is not the words that form prayer, but our union with the Divine Will; and then all is sacred, holy, and prayer within us. And then, peace is the eye of our acts, and therefore it will show you how to love Jesus and make Him loved.

Don Benedetto returns your wishes and blesses you. Pray for me, as I need it very much. I leave you closed in the Fiat; be careful not ever to leave It, and I ask the dear Baby to bless you.

Your most affectionate aunt,

the little daughter of the Divine Will

Corato, December 25, 1935

Fiat – In Voluntate Dei!

My good and reverend Mother Paolina,

(…) Now let's come to us, my good mother. I delayed writing you in order to let Holy Christmas draw near and then send you my poor wishes. But what can I, poor little ignorant, wish to you? So I ask dear Baby Jesus that He Himself bring you my sincere wishes. During these days, you will prepare your heart in order to form it as a host in which the Divine Infant will come to be reborn in you, and will bring you, as a wish and a gift, the heartbeat and the word of the Fiat, His baby tears, His tender moans and wails, in order to be consoled and to receive your tender love in return. My Mother, welcome Him soon, soothe His crying, warm Him, and be attentive so that He may always remain with you. This is what the Celestial Baby wants: He comes to remain with you. I am sure that you will not send Him back, and He will make of you His Royal Palace, His little Paradise. This is the wish I am sending you; I believe you will be content.

Now, this wish of mine – I extend it to my dear daughter, sister Remigia; I recommend that she be attentive so as to form the little paradise to the Little God. And I beg, I implore, sister Salette, sister Amelia and the whole community – each to form, not a star, but a Royal Palace for the dear Baby, and make Him a little fire, and the life of His Will. O, how happy will He feel in finding many royal palaces for His birth!

I send to all the greetings of the Divine Fiat, so that It may invest you with Its Light, cover your miseries with Its Love, and, if some of you are in pain, bring you balm and strength in order to convert everything into Will of God.

Now I expect your wishes and your prayers. Most dear Mother, I leave you in the Divine Volition to make yourself a saint and to enjoy the Christmas holidays. I kiss your right hand, and with respectful regards, I say,

the little daughter of the Divine Will

Corato, December 10, 1936

27. To Mother Cecilia

Fiat – In Voluntate Dei!

My good Mother Cecilia,

Thank you for everything. I don't know how to repay you, but I believe that Jesus will do it for me. I am sorry for your illness, since sight is so necessary. But the Divine Fiat is that which must embrace us, enclose us within Itself, in such a way as to consume us completely in the Divine Will. In fact, you must know that when we really decide always to do the Divine Will, His love is so great that He covers all our past miseries, defects and passions, as if we were newly reborn, and therefore, as though having made us new again, He wants to see nothing but His Will in us.

Now I send you my Christmas wishes in advance; I entrust you to Baby Jesus. During these days, make of your heart a little host, and dear Little Jesus will bring you as His wish, His love, His baby tears, His wails, His whole life, and will infuse in you His tender and compassionate love for His pains as a baby. This is my wish, and I also wish the whole community, especially those who remember me, the rebirth of Baby Jesus within their hearts.

I commend myself to your prayers, and from the heart, I will also do it for you; and leaving you in the arms of the Divine Volition, as though harmonizing, to breathe with one breath, with one heartbeat, with one will, I kiss your right hand with profound obsequies,

the little daughter of the Divine Will.

38. To a Religious

Fiat – In Voluntate Dei!

Reverend Mother,

I hope you are doing better. Just as dear Jesus brought you sufferings in order to continue a little bit of His life in you, now I hope that the Celestial Baby, with His childlike smiles, brings you sanctity, in order to continue the life of His works in your Maternity. And since our sufferings are in the hands of Jesus, they are files which sharpen us up more in sanctity, brushes that embellish us, love that consumes us. Dear Little Baby will come all festive, to reward you for the pains you have suffered, and will remain in you to dwell in you forever, bringing you the Divine Will as gift. This is the most beautiful wish I can send you; I think you will like it.

In this night of Holy Christmas, let us say, from the heart, a big and repeated "Fiat". In this way we will prepare a feast for the Divine Little One and He will bring us His own, so we will celebrate together His adorable birth… Now, I braid all the daughters together with the mother and I send my wishes to all, by praying to the Divine Infant that He will bring His Fiat to all the sisters, giving you the kiss of the Fiat (…)

66. To Sister Remigia

J.M.J.

Fiat! – In Voluntate Dei!

My good daughter Sister Remigia,

Thank you for your little letter; I appreciated it so much. May dear Jesus reward you by forming His life in you. However, it takes great attention: first of all you must try to have the necessary food in order to nourish dear Jesus and let Him grow. The first necessary food is peace. Disturbance is not food for Jesus. Peace forms the day, and converts everything we do into love. With it, we form abundant and divine material in order to form Jesus, nourish Him, and make Him grow. Once we have formed the necessary substance, the divine Will invests it and forms the Life of His Will. O, how happy He becomes then! Jesus finds in us His Will that loves Him, courts Him, and keeps Him in feast. Ant then what happens, my daughter? Our breath, our heartbeat and motion become the breath, the heartbeat and the motion of Jesus; we receive His life, we make of It our model, and all our acts are modeled by the Life of Jesus.

Therefore, be attentive; love peace and everything will smile at you, also Jesus Himself. This is my wish for Holy Christmas: be good, make yourself a saint, let all things be Will of God for you. With this, having a Divine Will in your power, how many beautiful and good things will you not be able to do? Everything. Pray for me; and leaving you in the eternal waves of the Divine Will, I say,

Your most affectionate aunt,

Luisa, the little daughter of the Divine Will.

Corato, December 1938

91. To Mother Cecilia

Fiat

My good and reverend Mother…

Here I am to give you my wishes for Holy Christmas. And what better wish to give you than send you little Jesus, so that He may make you be born together with Him? O, how He longs for it, and reaches the point of crying, because He does not want to be alone, but wants the creature to be born and live together with Him. The dear Baby will say to you, to the ear of your heart: "My daughter, let me live in you; do everything together with Me, and I will give you my Sanctity to make you a saint, my Beauty to embellish you, my Wisdom so that everything may be order within you. Then I will give you the great gift of my Will to let you breathe, palpitate, love, together with Me."… He will tell you: "Only then will I be content, when I see that you look like Me in everything."

My dearest Mother, let us make Jesus content; let us be born with Him and live together with Him. He is newly born, and does not want to be alone; He feels the need of the company of someone to kiss Him and dry His tears. My Mother, this is my wish; I believe that your Maternity will be content… More so, since every additional act we do in the Divine Will is a new birth for us. We are reborn in Jesus, and He in us. In this way we will make little Jesus happy.

Leaving you to be reborn together with Jesus, I kiss your right hand.

The little daughter of the Divine Will.

116. To Sister Mercede

My good and reverend Mother,

Thank you for all your attentions. As the Divine Will is known more, you will be able to expand Its interminable boundaries within your soul, and will make our Highest Good happy. My Mother, this is the only happiness of Jesus: that the soul live in His Will, because He can give whatever He wants, and can make of her one of the greatest portents of sanctity. He recognizes her as His daughter, and gives her His own Divine Will as her dwelling. He makes her share in all His goods, and in each one of her acts He forms His Divine Life – as many Jesuses for as many acts we do. What happiness to be able to say: "If I live in the Divine Will, I will form the Divine Generation within my acts, which will love Jesus with His own love. Not only this, but they will love Him in all hearts, and even in the Saints and in the Queen of Heaven." We will be the bearers of the love of all to our Creator.

Dearest Mother, Christmas is near, and I anticipate my wishes by wishing you the Divine Generation in your acts – the only purpose for which we were created. God gives us the place of honor in His Will, in order to give us His likeness and say: "My daughter is like me in everything…" May the Celestial Baby be enclosed in your heart, to form, He Himself, this Generation, all divine and celestial.

(…) I leave you in the Divine Volition as your refuge, help and defense.

Most affectionately yours,

The little daughter of the Divine Will

Corato, November 11, 1942

CHRISTMAS REFLECTIONS FROM THE VIRGIN MARY IN THE KINGDOM OF THE DIVINE WILL

The Doors of Heaven open, the Sun of the Eternal Word places Itself on the lookout and sends Its Angel to tell the Virgin that the Hour of God has come.

Now, my child, listen to me. I continued my life in Nazareth; the Divine Fiat continued to expand Its Kingdom in me. It used my most tiny acts, even the most indifferent ones – such as keeping the little house in order, starting the fire, sweeping, and all the acts which are usual in families – to let me feel Its life palpitating in the fire, in the water, in the food, in the air I breathed – in everything. And investing my little acts, It formed over them seas of light, of grace, of sanctity, because wherever It reigns, the Divine Will has the power of forming, even from little trifles, new heavens of enchanting beauty. Being immense, It does not how to do little things, but with Its power It gives value to trifles, making of them the greatest things, such as to astonish Heaven and earth. Everything is holy, everything is sacred, for one who lives from the Divine Will.

Now, child of my heart, pay attention to me and listen: several days before the descent of the Eternal Word upon earth, I could see the heavens opened and the Sun of the Divine Word at its doors, as though to look out for the one upon whom He was to take His flight, to render Himself celestial prisoner of one creature. Oh, how beautiful it was to see Him at the doors of Heaven, as though on the lookout to spy the fortunate creature who was to host her Creator! The Divine Persons of the Most Holy Trinity no longer looked at the earth as estranged to them, because there was little Mary, who, by possessing the Divine Will, had formed Its Divine Kingdom; Mary, in whom the Word could descend safely, as if into His own residence, in which He could find Heaven and the many suns of the many acts of Divine Will done within my soul. The Divinity overflowed with love, and removing the mantle of Justice which They had worn with the creature for so many centuries, the Divine Persons covered Themselves with the mantle of infinite mercy, and decreed among Themselves the descent of the Word. They were in the act of sounding the hour of the fulfillment. At this sound, Heaven and earth were astounded, and all stood all attention, to be spectators of such a great excess of love, and a prodigy so unheard-of.

Your Mama felt ignited with love, and echoing the love of my Creator, I wanted to form one single sea of love, so that the Word might descend upon earth within it. My prayers were incessant, and while I was praying in my little room, an angel came, sent from Heaven as messenger of the great King. He came before me, and bowing, he hailed me: "Hail, O Mary, our Queen; the Divine Fiat has filled you with grace. He has already pronounced His Fiat, for He wants to descend; He is just behind my shoulders, but He wants your Fiat to form the fulfillment of His Fiat."

At such a great announcement, so much desired by me – although I had never thought I was to be the chosen one – I was stupefied and I hesitated one instant. But the angel of the Lord told me: "Do not fear, our Queen, for you have found grace before God. You have conquered your Creator; therefore, to complete the victory – pronounce your Fiat."

I pronounced my Fiat, and – oh, marvel! The two Fiat fused together and the Divine Word descended into Me. My Fiat, receiving the same value as the Divine Fiat, from the seed of my humanity, formed the tiny little humanity which was to enclose the Word, and so the great prodigy of the Incarnation was accomplished.

O, power of the Supreme Fiat! You raised me so high as to render me powerful, to the point of being able to create within myself that humanity which was to enclose the Eternal Word, Whom Heaven and earth could not contain! The heavens were shaken, and all creation assumed the attitude of feast. Exulting with joy, they echoed around the little house of Nazareth, to give homage and obsequies to the Creator made man; and in their mute language, they said: "O, prodigy of prodigies, which only a God can do! Immensity has become little, power has become powerless, His unreachable height lowered itself to the abyss of the womb of a Virgin, and He is little and immense, powerful and powerless, strong and weak – at the same time!"

My dear child, you cannot comprehend what your Mama felt in the act of the Incarnation of the Word. Everyone yearned for and awaited my Fiat, which I could call omnipotent.

Now, dear child, listen to me: how much you should take to your heart doing the Divine Will and living from It! My power still exists: let me pronounce my Fiat over your soul. But in order to do this, I want your own. One alone cannot do true good; the greatest works are always done between two. God Himself did not want to do it by Himself, but wanted me together with Him, in order to form the great prodigy of the Incarnation. In my Fiat, and in Theirs was the life of the Man God formed; the destiny of mankind was restored, Heaven was no longer closed, and all goods were enclosed between the two Fiat. Therefore, let us say together, "Fiat! Fiat!", and within my maternal love I will enclose in you the life of the Divine Will.

Enough for now; tomorrow I will wait for you again, to narrate to my child what followed the Incarnation.

In Her Ardor of Love, Feeling as the Mother of Jesus, Mary goes on in search for Hearts to be Sanctified. Visit to St. Elisabeth; Sanctification of John.

As I became Mother of Jesus and your Mother, my seas of love redoubled, and, unable to contain them all, I felt the need to pour them out, and to be the first bearer of Jesus to the creatures, even at the cost of great sacrifices. But, what am I saying – sacrifices? When one really loves, sacrifices and pains are refreshments; they are reliefs and outpourings of the love one possesses. Oh, my child, if you do not feel the good of sacrifice, if you do not feel how it brings the most intimate joys, it is a sign that the divine love does not fill all your soul, and therefore that the Divine Will does not reign as Queen in you. It alone gives such strength to the soul as to render her invincible and capable of bearing any pain.

Place your hand upon your heart, and observe how many voids of love there are in it. Reflect: that secret self-esteem, your being disturbed by every slightest adversity, those little attachments you feel to things and to people, that tiredness in good, that bother caused by that which you don't like, are equivalent to as many voids of love within your heart; voids which, like little fevers, deprive you of the strength and of the desire to be filled with Divine Will. Oh, how you too will feel the refreshing and conquering virtue in your sacrifices, if you fill these voids with love!

My child, give me your hands now, and follow me, as I continue to give you my lessons.

So I departed from Nazareth, accompanied by Saint Joseph, facing a long journey, and crossing mountains to go visit Elisabeth in Judea, who, in her advanced age, had miraculously become a mother.

I went to her, not to make a simple visit, but because I burned with the desire to bring her Jesus. The fullness of grace, love and light which I felt in me, pushed me to bring, to multiply – to increase a hundredfold the life of my Son in creatures.

Yes, my child, the love of Mother which I had for all men, and for you in particular, was so great that I felt the extreme need to give my dear Jesus to everyone, that all might possess Him and love Him. The right of Mother, given to me by the Fiat, enriched me with such power as to multiply Jesus as many times as there are creatures who want to receive Him. This was the greatest miracle I could perform: to have Jesus ready to give to whomever desired Him. How happy I felt!

How I wish that you too, my child, in approaching and visiting people, would always be the bearer of Jesus, capable of making Him known, and yearning to make Him loved.

After many days of travel, we finally arrived in Judea, and I hastened to the house of Elisabeth. She came toward me in feast. At the greeting I gave her, marvelous phenomena occurred. My little Jesus exulted in my womb, and fixing little John in the womb of his mother with the rays of His Divinity, He sanctified him, gave him the use of reason, and let him know that He was the Son of God. And John started so vigorously with love and joy that Elisabeth was shaken; touched by the light of the Divinity of my Son, she too recognized that I had become the Mother of God. And in the emphasis of her love, trembling with gratitude, she exclaimed: "How to me, so much honor, that the Mother of the Lord would come to me?"

I did not deny the highest mystery; rather, I humbly confirmed it. Praising God with the song of the Magnificat – sublime canticle, through which the Church continuously honors me, I announced that the Lord had done great things in me, His servant, and that because of this, all people would call me blessed.

My child, I felt devoured with the desire to pour out the flames of love that consumed me, and to reveal my secret to Elisabeth, who also longed for the Messiah to come upon earth. A secret is a need of the heart which is revealed, irresistibly, to people who are capable of understanding each other.

Who can ever tell you how much good my visit brought to Elisabeth, to John, and to their house? Everyone was sanctified, filled with gladness, felt unusual joys, and comprehended things unheard-of. John, in particular, received all the graces which were necessary for him, to prepare himself to be the Precursor of my Son.

Dearest child, the Divine Will does great and unheard-of things wherever It reigns. If I worked many prodigies, it was because It had Its royal place in me. If you let the Divine Will reign in your soul, you too will become the bearer of Jesus to the creatures – you too will feel the irresistible need to give Him to all!

The Virgin is a Heaven studded with Stars. In This Heaven the Sun of the Divine Fiat blazes with Its Most Refulgent Rays, filling Heaven and earth. Jesus in the Womb of His Mama

My dear child, today I await you more than ever. My maternal heart is swollen – I feel the need to pour out my ardent love with my child: I want to say to you that I am the Mother of Jesus. My joys are infinite; seas of happiness inundate me. I can say: I am the Mother of Jesus; His creature, His servant, is Mother of Jesus – and I owe this only to the Fiat. It rendered me full of grace; It prepared the worthy dwelling for my

Creator. Therefore, always glory, honor and thanksgiving be to the Supreme Fiat.

Now listen to me, child of my heart. As soon as the little humanity of Jesus was formed in my womb by the power of the Supreme Fiat, the sun of the Eternal Word incarnated Himself in it. I had my heaven, formed by the Fiat, all studded with most refulgent stars which glittered with Joys, beatitudes, harmonies of divine beauty; and the sun of the Eternal Word, refulgent with inaccessible light, came to take His place within this heaven, hidden in His little humanity. And unable to contain it, the center of this sun remained in It, but its light overflowed outside, and investing Heaven and earth, it reached every heart; with the pounding of its light, it knocked at every creature, and with voices of penetrating light, it said to them: "My children, open to me; give me a place in your heart. I have descended from Heaven to earth in order to form my life in each one of you. My Mother is the center in which I reside, and all my children will be the circumference, in which I want to form so many of my lives for as many as are my children."

And the light knocked, over and over again, without ever ceasing, while the little humanity of Jesus was moaning, crying, and longing; making His tears, His moans and His pangs of love and pain flow within that light which reached into the hearts.

Now, you must know that your Mama began a new life. I was aware of everything that my Son did. I saw Him devoured by seas of flames of love; each one of His heartbeats, breaths and pains, were seas of love that He unleashed, with which He enveloped all creatures to make them His own by force of love and suffering. In fact, you must know that as His little humanity was conceived, He conceived all the pains He was to suffer, up to the last day of His life. He enclosed all souls within Himself, because, being God, no one could escape Him. His immensity enclosed all creatures, His all-seeingness rendered them all present to Him. Therefore, my Jesus, my Son, felt the weight and the burden of all sins of each creature. And I, your Mama, followed Him in everything, and felt within my maternal heart this new generation of the pains of my Jesus, and the new generation of all the souls, whom, as Mother, I was to generate with Jesus to the grace, to the light and to the new life which my dear Son came to bring upon earth.

My child, you must know that from the moment I was conceived, I loved you as mother, I felt you within my heart, I burned with love for you, but I did not know why. The Divine Fiat made me do things, but kept their secret hidden from me. But as He incarnated himself, He revealed the secret to me, and I understood the fecundity of my maternity – as I was to be not only Mother of Jesus, but Mother of all. This maternity was to be formed on the stake of suffering and of love. My child, how much I loved you, and do love you!

Now listen, dear child, to the point one can reach, when the Divine Will takes operating life in the creature, and the human will lets It work, without impeding Its step. This Fiat, which by nature possesses the generative virtue, generates all goods in the creature: It renders her fecund, giving her maternity over all – over all goods, and over the One Who created her. Maternity says and means true love: heroic love – love which is content with dying to give life to the one it has generated. Without this, the word maternity is sterile, it is empty, and is reduced to a mere word, but does not exist in fact. Therefore, my child, if you want the generation of all goods, let the Fiat take Its operating life in you, which will give you maternity, and you will love everyone with the love of a mother. And I, your Mama, will teach you how to fecundate this maternity, all holy and divine, within you.

Rising Sun. Full Day: the Eternal Word in our Midst.

Dearest child, do not fear. Trust your Mama, pour everything into my heart, and I will take everything into account. I will be your Mama; I will change your pains into light, and will use them to expand the boundaries of the Kingdom of the Divine Will within your soul.

So, put everything aside for now, and listen to me. I want to tell you what little king Jesus worked in my maternal womb, and how your Mama did not lose even one breath of little Jesus.

My child, the little humanity of Jesus continued to grow, united hypostatically with the Divinity. My maternal womb was very narrow – obscure; there was not a glimmer of light, and I saw Him in my maternal womb, immobile, enwrapped in a deep night. But do you know what formed this obscurity, so intense, for the infant Jesus? The human will, in which man had voluntarily enwrapped himself, and for as many sins as he committed, so many abysses of darkness did he form around and within himself, in such a way as to be rendered immobile in doing good. And so my dear Jesus, in order to put to flight the darkness of such a deep night, in which man had made himself the prisoner of his own tenebrous will – to the point of losing the motion of doing good – chose the sweet prison of His Mama and, voluntarily, exposed Himself to immobility for nine months.

My child, if you knew how martyred was my maternal heart in seeing little Jesus immobile, crying and sighing in my little womb! His ardent heartbeat palpitated very strongly and was fidgety with love; He made His heartbeat heard in every heart, to ask – for pity's sake – for their own souls, to enclose them in the light of His Divinity, because for love of them He had voluntarily exchanged the light for darkness so that all might obtain true light in order to reach safety.

My dearest child, who can tell you what my little Jesus suffered in my womb? Unheard-of and indescribable pains! He was endowed with full reason – He was God and man – and His love was so great that it was as if He put aside the infinite seas of joys, of happiness, of light, and plunged His tiny Humanity into the seas of darkness, of bitterness, of unhappiness and miseries, which the creatures had prepared for Him. And little Jesus took them all upon His shoulders, as if they were His own. My child, true love never says 'enough'. It does not look at pains, and through pains it searches for the loved one – only then is it content, when it gives its own life to give life back to the beloved.

My child, listen to your Mama; do you see what a great evil it is to do your will? Not only do you prepare a night for your Jesus and for yourself, but you form seas of bitterness, of unhappiness and of miseries, in which you remain so engulfed as to be unable to escape. Therefore, be attentive; make me happy by saying to me: "I want always to do the Divine Will."

Now listen, my child; little Jesus, in spasms of love, was in the act of taking the step to come out to the light of the day. His anxieties, His ardent sighs and desires to embrace the creature, to make Himself seen, and to look at her in order to enrapture her to Himself, gave Him no more rest. And just as one day He had put Himself on the lookout at the doors of heaven in order to enclose Himself in my womb, so was He now in the act of putting Himself on the lookout at the doors of my womb, which was more than heaven. The sun of the Eternal Word rises in the world and forms in it the full day. There will be night no longer for poor creatures, nor dawn, nor daybreak – but always sun, more than at the fullness of the day.

Your Mama felt she could no longer contain Him within herself. Seas of light and love inundated me, and just as I conceived Him within a sea of light, within a sea of light He came out of my maternal womb. Dear child, for one who lives of Divine Will everything is light, and everything converts into light.

Enraptured in this light, I awaited to hug my little Jesus in my arms, and as he came out of my womb, I heard His first loving wailings. The angel of the Lord placed Him in my arms and I squeezed Him very tightly to my heart; I gave Him my first kiss and little Jesus gave me His. Enough for now; tomorrow I will wait for you again, to continue the narration of the birth of Jesus.

Little King Jesus is Born. The Angels point to Him and call the Shepherds to adore Him. Heaven and Earth rejoice, and the Sun of the Eternal Word, following Its Course, Dispels the Night of Sin, and gives start to the Full Day of Grace. The Home of Bethlehem.

My dearest child, oh, how I long for you to come into my arms, to have the great contentment of being able to say to our little baby king: "Don't cry, my pretty one. See, here with us is my little child, who wants to recognize you as king and give you dominion within her soul, to let you lay in her the Kingdom of your Will."

Now, child of my heart, while you are all attentive in longing for little baby Jesus, pay attention to me and listen. You must know that it was midnight when the little newborn king came out from my maternal womb. The night turned into day; the one who was the lord of light put to flight the night of the human will, the night of sin, the night of all evils; and as a sign of what He was doing in the order of souls with His usual omnipotent Fiat, the midnight turned into most refulgent daylight. All created things ran to praise their Creator in that little humanity. The sun ran to give its first kisses of light to little baby Jesus, and warm Him with its heat; the ruling wind purified the air of the stable with Its waves, and with its sweet moaning said to Him: "I love you"; the heavens were shaken from their very foundations; the earth exulted and trembled down to the abyss; the sea roared with its gigantic waves. In sum, all created things recognized that their Creator was in their midst, and they all competed in praising Him. The very angels, forming light in the air, with melodious voices which all could hear, said: "Glory to God in the highest, and peace on earth to men of good will! The celestial baby is born in the grotto of Bethlehem, wrapped in poor little swaddling clothes…" – so much so, that the shepherds who were in vigil, listened to the angelic voices and ran to visit the little divine king.

My dear child, continue to listen to me. As I received Him into my arms and gave Him my first kiss, I felt the need of love to give something of my own to my little Son; and offering Him my breast, I gave Him abundant milk – milk formed in my person by the Divine Fiat Itself, in order to nourish little king Jesus. But who can tell you what I felt in doing this, and the seas of grace, of love, of sanctity, that my Son gave to me in return? Then I wrapped Him in poor but clean little clothes, and I placed Him in the manger. This was His Will, and I could do not without executing it. But before doing this, I shared Him with dear Saint Joseph, placing Him into his arms. O, how he rejoiced; he squeezed Him to his heart, and the sweet little baby poured torrents of graces into his soul. Then, together with Saint Joseph, we fixed a little hay in the manger, and detaching Him from my maternal arms, I laid Him in it. Your Mama, enraptured by the beauty of the divine infant, remained kneeling before Him most of the time. I put all my seas of love into motion, which the Divine Will had formed in me, to love Him, adore Him, and thank Him.

And what did the little celestial baby do in the manger? A continuous act of the Will of our celestial Father, which was also His. Moaning and sighing, He wailed, cried and called to everyone, saying in His loving wailing: "Come, you all, children of mine; for love of you I am born to suffering and to tears. Come all of you, to know the excess of my love! Give Me shelter in your hearts. And there were shepherds, coming and going, to visit Him, and to all He gave His sweet gaze and His loving smile, even within His tears.

Now, my child, a little word to you: You must know that my whole joy was to hold my dear Son Jesus on my lap, but the Divine Will made me understand that I should place Him in the manger, at everyone's disposal, so that whoever wanted, could caress Him, kiss Him, and take Him in their arms, as if He were their own. He was the little king of all; therefore, they had the right to make of Him a sweet pledge of love. And I, in order to fulfill the Supreme Volition, deprived myself of my innocent joys, beginning, with works and sacrifices, the office of Mother – giving Him to all.

My child, the Divine Will is demanding and wants everything, even the sacrifice of the holiest things; and according to circumstances, even the great sacrifice of depriving oneself of Jesus. However, It does so in order to extend Its kingdom even more, and to multiply the life of Jesus Himself; because when the creature deprives herself of Him out of love for Him, her heroism and sacrifice is so great that she has the virtue of producing a new life of Jesus, in order to form another home for Jesus. Therefore, dear child, be attentive, and never deny anything to the Divine Will, under any pretext.

Here sounds the First Hour of Sorrow. A Star, with mute Voice, calls the Magi to adore Jesus. A Prophet reveals the Sorrows of the Sovereign Queen

My dearest child, how happy I am to have you close to me, to be able to teach you how the Kingdom of the Divine Will can lay Itself in all things. All crosses, sorrows and humiliations, invested by the life of the Divine Fiat, are like raw material in Its hands, in order to nourish Its Kingdom and extend It more and more.

Therefore, pay attention to me, and listen to your Mama. I continued my stay in the grotto of Bethlehem with Jesus and dear Saint Joseph. How happy we were! Through the presence of the divine infant and of the Divine Will operating in us, that little grotto had changed into paradise. It is true that pains and tears were not lacking, but compared to the immense seas of joy, of happiness and of light which the Divine Fiat made arise in each one of our acts, they were just little drops plunged into these seas. And then, the sweet and lovable presence of my dear Son was a happiness of the greatest kind.

Now, dear child, you must know that the eighth day arrived after the birth of the celestial baby into the light of the day, and the Divine Fiat sounded the hour of sorrow, ordering us to circumcise the charming little baby. It was a most painful cut which little Jesus had to go through. It was the law of those times that all the firstborn had to undergo this painful cut. It can be called the law of sin, but my Son was innocent and His law was the law of love; in spite of all this, since He came to find, not the man king, but the decayed man, in order to become brother and to raise him, He wanted to lower Himself, submitting Himself to the law.

My child, Saint Joseph and I felt a shiver of pain, but fearless and without hesitation, we called the Minister and we had Him circumcised with a most painful cut. In the bitter pain, baby Jesus cried and flung Himself into my arms, asking for help. Saint Joseph and I blended our tears with His; we gathered the first blood shed by Jesus for love of the creatures; we gave Him the name of Jesus – powerful name – which was to make Heaven and earth tremble, and even hell; a name which was to be balm, defense and help for every heart.

Now, my child, this cut was the image of the cruel cut that man had made to his own soul by doing his own will; and my dear Son allowed Himself to receive this cut in order to heal that hard cut of the human wills – to heal with His blood the wounds of the many sins that the poison of the human will has caused in the creatures. Every act of human will is a cut which is inflicted, and a wound that is opened; and the celestial baby, with His most painful cut, prepared the remedy for all the human wounds.

Now, my child, another surprise: a new star shines under the vault of the heavens, and with its light it is searching for adorers, to lead them to recognize and adore baby Jesus. Three individuals, each distant from the other, are touched by it, and invested by supernatural light, follow the star, which leads them to the grotto of Bethlehem, to the feet of the baby Jesus. What was not the astonishment of these Magi Kings, in recognizing in that divine infant the King of Heaven and earth – the One Who had come to love and to save all? In fact, when the Magi were in the act of adoring Him, enraptured by that celestial beauty, the newborn baby made His Divinity shine forth from His little humanity, and the grotto turned into paradise; so much so, that they were not able to separate themselves from the feet of the divine infant – not before He again withdrew the light of the Divinity within His humanity. And I, exercising the office of mother, spoke at length of the descent of the Word, and fortified them in faith, hope and charity, symbolized by the gifts offered to Jesus. Then, full of joy, they withdrew to their regions, to be the first propagators.

My dear child, do not move from my side; follow me everywhere. Forty days from the birth of little King Jesus are about to sound – when the Divine Fiat calls us to the temple in order to fulfill the law of the Presentation of my Son. So, we went to the temple. It was the first time that we went out together with my sweet baby. A vein of sorrow opened in my heart: I was going to offer Him as victim for the salvation of all! We entered the temple, and first we adored the Divine Majesty; then we called the priest, and placing Him in his arms, I made the offering of the celestial baby to the eternal Father – offering Him in sacrifice for the salvation of all. The priest was Simeon, and as I placed Him in his arms, he recognized that He was the Divine Word and exulted with immense joy; and after the offering, assuming the attitude of prophet, he prophesied all my sorrows... O, how the Supreme Fiat sounded over my maternal heart – thoroughly, with vibrating sound, the cruel tragedy of all the pains of my little Son! But that which pierced me the most were the words that the holy prophet said to me: "This dear baby will be the salvation and ruin of many, and will be the target of contradictions."

If the Divine Will had not sustained me, I would have died instantly of pure pain. But It gave me life, and used it to form in me the Kingdom of sorrows, within the Kingdom of Its Will.

Therefore, in addition to the right of Mother which I had over all, I acquired the right of Mother and Queen of all Sorrows. Ah, yes, with my sorrows, I acquired the little coin to pay the debts of my children, and even those of the ungrateful children.

Now, my child, you must know that in the light of the Divine Will I already knew all the sorrows I was to suffer – and even more than that which the holy prophet had told me. But in that act, so solemn, of offering my own Son – in hearing it all being repeated to me – I felt so pierced that my heart bled, and deep lacerations opened in my soul.

Now, listen to your Mama: in your sufferings, in the painful encounters which are not lacking for you, never lose heart; but with heroic love let the Divine Will assume Its royal place in your pains, so that It may convert them into little coins of infinite value, with which you will be able to pay the debts of your brothers – to ransom them from the slavery of the human will, and make them enter again, as free children, into the Kingdom of the Divine Will.

Here sounds the First Hour of Sorrow. Heroism in submitting the Infant Jesus to the Cruel Cut of Circumcision.

Dearest child, how I long for your company, to narrate to you our story of love and of sorrow! Company renders joy more sweet, gentle and dear, while sorrow is mitigated and compensated by the company of the one who loves us.

Now, you must know that only eight days had passed from the birth of the divine infant. Everything was feast and happiness; the very creation, taking a festive attitude, celebrated Its baby Creator. But duty interrupted our joys, because in those times there was a law that all firstborn sons were to undergo the cruel cut of circumcision. My heart of a Mother bled with sorrow in having to submit my dear Son, my Life, my own Creator, to such a bitter pain. O, how I would have wanted to take His place! But the Supreme Volition imposed Itself on my love, and giving me heroism, commanded me to circumcise the baby God. My child, you cannot understand how much it cost me; but the Divine Fiat won, and I obeyed, united with Saint Joseph. In mutual agreement, we had my little Son circumcised. At the painful cut, I felt my heart torn, and I cried. Saint Joseph cried too, and my dear baby sobbed, and His pain was such that He shivered and looking at me, He asked for help. What an hour of pain and spasm for the three of us! It was such that, more than a sea, it engulfed all creatures, bringing them the first pledge and even the Life of my Son to take them to safety.

Now, blessed child, you must know that this cut enclosed profound mysteries: first, it was the seal that His brotherhood with the whole human family impressed in the little humanity of the celestial baby; and the blood He shed was the first disbursement before the Divine Justice in order to ransom all human generations. The dear baby was innocent; He was not obliged by the law. But He wanted to submit Himself, first, to give example; and then, to give trust and courage, saying to all: "Do not fear; I am your little brother, similar to you. Let us love one another, and I will bring you all to safety. I will bring you all to my Celestial Father, as my dear brothers."

My child, what an example the celestial baby gives! He, Who is the Author of the law, obeys the law. He is born only eight days ago, yet He takes it as a duty, submitting Himself to the cruel cut of circumcision; an indelible cut – as indelible as the union He has come to form with degraded humanity. This says that sanctity is in doing one's own duty, in the observance of the laws, and in doing the Divine Will. Sanctity without duty does not exist. It is duty that places order, harmony, and the seal on sanctity.

Furthermore, my child, you must know that as Adam withdrew from the Divine Will, after his short life of innocence, his human will was wounded, more than by a deadly knife, and through this wound entered sin and passions. He lost the beautiful day of the Divine Will, and was so degraded as to move to pity. So, after the joys of His birth, my dear Son wanted to be circumcised, so that His wound might heal the wound that Adam made in Himself by doing his own will. And with His blood, He prepared for him the bath, to wash him of all his sins, to strengthen Him and to embellish him, in such a way as to render him worthy to receive again that Divine Will he had rejected, which formed his sanctity and his happiness. Child, there was not one work or pain He suffered, which did not seek to reorder again the Divine Will in creatures.

Therefore, in all circumstances, even the painful and humiliating ones, take to heart doing the Divine Will in everything, because these are the raw material in which It hides in order to operate in the creature, and to let her acquire His life acting in the creature.

Now, dearest child, in so much pain, the most beautiful joy arises, such as to stop our tears. As He was circumcised, we gave Him the Most Holy Name of Jesus, wanted by the angel. In pronouncing this Most Holy Name, the joy, the contentment, was such as to sweeten our sorrow. More so, since in this name, all those who wanted, would find balm for their pains, defense in dangers, victory in temptations, a hand, so as not to fall into sin, and the medicine to all their evils. This Most Holy Name of Jesus makes hell tremble; the angels revere It, and It sounds sweet to the ear of the Celestial Father. Before this name, all bow down and adore. Powerful name, holy name, great name; whoever invokes It with faith will feel marvels – the miraculous secret of the virtue of this Most Holy name.

Now, my child, I recommend to you: pronounce always this name, "Jesus". When you see that your human will, weak and vacillating, hesitates in doing the Divine, the name of Jesus will make it rise again in the Divine Fiat. If you are oppressed, call upon Jesus; if you work, call upon Jesus; if you sleep, call upon Jesus; and when you wake up, may your first word be "Jesus". Call Him always; it is a name that contains seas of grace, which He gives to those who call Him and love Him.

The Divine Fiat calls Her to the Heroic Sacrifice of offering Baby Jesus for the Salvation of Mankind. The Purification.

Dearest child, how happy I am to have you near me! My maternal heart feels the need to pour my love out and to confide to you my secrets. Be attentive to my lessons, and listen to me. You must know that we have been forty days, now, in this grotto of Bethlehem, the first home of my Son down here; but, how many wonders in this grotto! The celestial infant, in an outpouring of love, descended from Heaven to earth; He was conceived, and was born – and felt the need to display this love. Each tear, wail and moan, was an outpouring of love; also, feeling numb with cold, His lips, livid and shivering – these were all outpourings of love that He displayed; and He looked for His Mama in order to deposit this love, which He could no longer contain, and I was prey to His love. I felt I was being continuously wounded, and I felt my dear little one palpitate, breathe and move within my maternal heart. I felt Him crying, moaning and wailing, and I remained inundated by the flames of His love. The circumcision had already opened deep wounds, into which He poured so much love that I felt Queen and Mother of love. I felt enraptured in seeing that in every pain, tear and movement of my sweet Jesus, He looked for and called upon His Mama, as the dear refuge of His acts and of His life. Who can tell you, my child, what passed between me and the celestial baby during these forty days? His acts repeated together with me, His tears, His pains, His love, were as though transfused – whatever He did, I did.

Now, at the end of the forty days, the dear baby, drowned more than ever in His love, wanted to obey the law, presenting Himself to the temple to offer Himself for the salvation of everyone. It was the Divine Will that called us to the great sacrifice, and we promptly obeyed. My child, when this Divine Fiat finds promptness in doing what It wants, It puts at the creature's disposal Its divine strength, Its sanctity, Its creative power to multiply that act – that sacrifice, for all, and for each one; It places in that sacrifice the little coin of infinite value, with which one can pay for, and satisfy for all.

It was the first time that your Mama and Saint Joseph went out together with baby Jesus. All creation recognized its Creator; they felt honored at having Him in their midst, and in a festive attitude, they accompanied us along the way. As we arrived at the temple, we prostrated ourselves and adored the Supreme Majesty. Then we placed Him in the arms of the priest, who was Simeon, who made of Him an offering to the Eternal Father – offering Him for the salvation of all. And while he offered Him, inspired by God, he recognized the Divine Word, and exulting with immense joy, he adored and thanked the dear baby. After the offering, he assumed the attitude of prophet, and predicted all of my sorrows. Oh, how painfully did the Supreme Fiat make my maternal heart feel, with vibrating sound, the cruel tragedy of all the pains which my divine Son was to suffer! Each word was a sharp sword that pierced me.

But that which pierced my heart the most was to hear that this celestial infant was to be, not only the salvation, but also the ruin of many, and the target of contradictions! What pain! What sorrow! If the Divine Will had not sustained me, I would have died instantly of pure pain. But It gave me life, to begin to form in me the Kingdom of Sorrows within the Kingdom of Its own Divine Will. Therefore, with the right of Mother which I had over all, I acquired also the right of Mother and Queen of all Sorrows. O, yes, with my sorrows, I acquired the little coin with which to pay the debts of my children, and also those of my ungrateful children.

Now, my child, you must know that through the light of the Divine Will which reigned in me, I already knew all the sorrows I was to suffer – and even more than those about which the holy Prophet told me. I can say that he prophesied for me the sorrows which I was to receive from the outside, but he said not a word on my interior pains, which were to pierce me even more, or the interior pains which passed between me and my Son. But in spite of this, in that act, so solemn, of the offering of my Son – in hearing them being repeated, I felt so pierced that my heart bled, and new veins of sorrow and deep wounds opened within my soul.

Now, listen to your Mama. In your pains, in the painful encounters which you also do not lack, and when you know that the Divine Will wants a sacrifice from you, be ready – do not lose heart, but rather, repeat quickly the dear and sweet Fiat : "Whatever You want, I want"; and with heroic love, let the Divine Will take Its royal place in your sufferings, that It may convert them into a little coin of infinite value, with which you will be able to pay your debts, as well as those of your brothers – to ransom them from the slavery of the human will, and to let them enter, as free children, into the Kingdom of the Divine Fiat. In fact, you must know that the Divine Will is so pleased by the sacrifice which It wanted of the creature, that It gives her all Its divine rights, and constitutes her queen of the sacrifice and of the good which will arise in the midst of creatures.

A New Star, with Its Sweet Glittering, calls the Magi to adore Jesus. The Epiphany.

Dearest child, you are right in saying that you see me as more beautiful. You must know that when I saw my Son being circumcised and His blood pouring from the wound, I loved that blood, that wound, and I became Mother twice: Mother of my Son, and Mother of His blood – of His cruel pain. Therefore I acquired a double right of maternity – a double right of graces before the Supreme Majesty, for myself and for all mankind. This is why you see me as more beautiful.

My child, how beautiful it is to do good, to suffer in peace for love of the One who created us. This binds the Divinity to the creature, and gives her so much grace and love – to the extent of drowning her. This love and these graces cannot remain idle, but want to run and give themselves to all, to make known the one who has given so much. This is why I felt the need to make my Son known.

Now, my blessed child, the Divinity, Who can deny nothing to one who loves It, makes a new star, more beautiful and radiant, arise under the blue heavens. And with its light, it goes in search of adorers, to say to the whole world, with its mute glittering: "The One Who has come to save you is born! Come to adore Him and to know Him as your Savior!"

But...human ingratitude! Among many, only three People paid attention, and without considering the sacrifices, put themselves on the path to follow the star. And just as a star guided their persons along the path, so also my prayers, my love, my sighs and my graces, in my desire of making known the Celestial Baby – the Awaited One from all centuries – like many stars descending into their hearts, illuminated their minds and guided their interiors, in such a way that, without yet knowing Him, they felt that they loved the One for whom they were looking, and they hastened their step in order to reach and see the One whom they so much loved.

My dearest child, my heart of a Mother rejoiced for the faithfulness, the correspondence and the sacrifice of these Magi Kings, to come to know and adore my Son. But I cannot hide from you a secret sorrow of mine: among many, only three. In the history of the centuries, how many times is this sorrow of mine and this human ingratitude not repeated! My Son and I do nothing but make stars arise, one more beautiful than the other, to call some to know their Creator, some to sanctity, some to rise again from sin, some to the heroism of a sacrifice... But do you want to know what these stars are? A painful encounter is a star; a truth that one comes to know is a star; a love unrequited by other creatures is a star; a setback, a suffering, a disillusion, an unexpected fortune, are many stars which shed light in the minds of creatures. Caressing them, they want to make them find the Celestial Infant, who is fidgeting with love, shivering with cold, and seeking a refuge in their hearts to be known and loved. But, alas, I who hold Him in my arms, wait in vain for the stars to bring me the creatures, in order to place Him in their hearts – and my maternity is restrained, hindered. While I am the Mother of Jesus, I am prevented from being the mother of all, because they are not around me, and do not look for Jesus. So the stars hide, and they remain in the Jerusalems of the world, without Jesus. What sorrow, my child, what sorrow! It takes correspondence, fidelity and sacrifice to follow the stars; and if the sun of the Divine Will rises within the soul – how much attention does it not take. Otherwise, one remains in the darkness of the human will.

Now, my child, as they entered Jerusalem, the holy Magi Kings lost the star, but, still, they did not stop looking for Jesus. But as they went outside the city, the star reappeared and led them, festive, into the grotto of Bethlehem. I received them with the love of a Mother, and the dear Baby looked at them with great love and majesty, letting His Divinity shine through His little humanity. Bowing down, they knelt at His feet, and adoring and contemplating that celestial Beauty, they recognized Him as true God. They remained enraptured, ecstatic – enjoying Him; so much so, that the Celestial Baby had to withdraw His Divinity into His Humanity, otherwise they would have remained there, unable to move from His divine feet.

Then, as they came round from their rapture, in which they offered the gold of their souls, the incense of their faith and adoration, the myrrh of all of their beings and of any sacrifice He might have wanted, they added the offering of the external gifts, symbol of their interior acts: gold, incense and myrrh. But my love of Mother was not yet content; I wanted to place the sweet Baby in their arms, and – oh, with how much love did they kiss Him and press Him to their chests! They felt paradise, in advance, within them. Through this, my Son bound all the gentile nations to the knowledge of the true God, and placed the goods of Redemption, the return to faith of all peoples, in common for all. He constituted Himself King of the dominators, and ruling over all, with the weapons of His love, of His pains and of His tears, He called the Kingdom of His Will upon earth. And I, your Mama, wanted to be the first apostle. I instructed them; I told them the story of my Son, of His ardent love; I recommended that they make Him known to all, and assuming the first place of Mother and Queen of all Apostles, I blessed them, I had them blessed by the dear Baby, and happy and in tears, they left again for their regions. I did not leave them, I accompanied them with maternal affection, and to repay them, I let them feel Jesus in their hearts. How happy they were! You must know that only when I see that my Son has dominion, possession, and forms His perennial dwelling in the hearts of those who search for Him and love Him – only then do I feel a true Mother.

Now a little word to you, my child: if you want me to act as your true Mother, let me place Jesus in your heart. You will make Him happy with your love; you will feed Him with the food of His Will, because He takes no other food; You will clothe Him with the sanctity of your works. And I will come into your heart, I will raise my dear child again together with you, and I will perform for you and for Him, the office of Mother. In this way, I will feel the pure joys of my maternal fecundity. You must know that anything which does not begin with Jesus, who is inside the heart – even though they may be the most beautiful works on the outside – cannot please me, because they are empty of the life of my dear Son.

APPENDIX

Biographical notes

The Servant of God Luisa Piccarreta was born in Corato in the Province of Bari, on April 23, 1865 and died there in the odor of sanctity on March 4, 1947.

Luisa had the good fortune to be born into one of those patriarchal families that still survive in our realm of Puglia and like to live deep in the country, peopling our farmhouses. Her parents, Vito Nicola and Rosa Tarantino, had five children: Maria, Rachele, Filomena, Luisa and Angela. Maria, Rachele and Filomena married. Angela, commonly called Angelina, remained single and looked after her sister until she died.

Luisa was born on the Sunday after Easter and was baptized that same day. Her father – a few hours after her birth – wrapped her in a blanket and carried her to the parish church where holy Baptism was administered to her.

Nicola Piccarreta was a worker on a farm belonging to the Mastrorilli family, located at the middle of Via delle Murge in a neighborhood called *Torre Disperata,* 27 kilometers from Corato. Those who know these places, set among the sunny, bare and stony hills, can appreciate the solemnity of the silence that envelops them. Luisa spent many years of her childhood and adolescence on this farm. In front of the old house, the impressive, centuries-old mulberry tree still stands, with the great hollow in its trunk where Luisa used to hide when she was little in order to pray, far from prying eyes. It was in this lonely, sunny spot place that Luisa's divine adventure began which was to lead her down the paths of suffering and holiness. Indeed, it was in this very place that she came to suffer unspeakably from the attacks of the devil who at times even tormented her physically. Luisa, to be rid of this suffering, turned ceaselessly to prayer, addressing in particular the Virgin Most Holy, who comforted her by her presence.

Divine Providence led the little girl down paths so mysterious that she knew no joys other than God and his grace. One day, in fact, the Lord said to her: "*I have gone round and round the world again and again, and I looked one by one at all my creatures to find the smallest one of all. Among so many I found you. Your littleness pleased me and I chose you; I entrusted you to my angels so that they would care for you, not to make you great, but to preserve your littleness, and now I want to begin the great work of fulfilling my will. Nor will you feel any greater through this, indeed it is my will to make you even smaller, and you will continue to be the little daughter of the Divine Will*" (cf. Volume XII, March 23, 1921).

When she was nine, Luisa received Jesus in the Eucharist for the first time and Holy Confirmation, and from that moment learned to remain for hours praying before the Blessed Sacrament. When she was eleven she wanted to enroll in the Association of the Daughters of Mary – flourishing at the time – in the Church of San Giuseppe. At the age of eighteen, Luisa became a Dominican Tertiary taking the name of Sr. Maddalena. She was one of the first to enroll in the Third Order, which her parish priest was promoting. Luisa's devotion to the Mother of God was to develop into a profound Marian spirituality, a prelude to what she would one day write about Our Lady.

Jesus' voice led Luisa to detachment from herself and from everyone. At about eighteen, from the balcony of her house in Via Nazario Sauro, she had a vision of Jesus suffering under the weight of the Cross, who raised his eyes to her saying: "*O soul, help me!*". From that moment an insatiable longing to suffer for Jesus and for the salvation of souls was enkindled in

Luisa. So began those physical sufferings which, in addition to her spiritual and moral sufferings, reached the point of heroism.

The family mistook these phenomena for sickness and sought medical help. But all the doctors consulted were perplexed at such an unusual clinical case. Luisa was subject to a state of corpse-like rigidity – although she showed signs of life – and no treatment could relieve her of this unspeakable torment. When all the resources of science had been exhausted, her family turned to their last hope: priests. An Augustinian priest, Fr. Cosma Loiodice, at home because of the Siccardian[*] laws, was summoned to her bedside: to the wonder of all present, the sign of the Cross which this priest made over the poor body, sufficed to restore her normal faculties instantly to the sick girl. After Fr. Loiodice had left for his friary, certain secular priests were called in who restored Luisa to normality with the sign of the Cross. She was convinced that all priests were holy, but one day the Lord told her: "*Not because they are all holy – indeed, if they only were! – but simply because they are the continuation of my priesthood in the world you must always submit to their priestly authority; never oppose them, whether they are good or bad*" (cf. Volume I). Throughout her life, Luisa was to be submissive to priestly authority. This was to be one of the greatest sources of her suffering. Her daily need for the priestly authority in order to return to her usual tasks was her deepest mortification. In the beginning, she suffered the most humiliating misunderstandings on the part of the priests themselves who considered her a lunatic filled with exalted ideas, who simply wanted to attract attention. Once they left her in that state for more than twenty days. Luisa, having accepted the role of victim, came to experience a most peculiar condition: every morning she found herself rigid, immobile, huddled up in bed, and no one was able to stretch her out, to raise her arms or move her head or legs. As we know, it required the presence of a priest who, by blessing her with the sign of the Cross, dispelled that corpse-like rigidity and enabled her to return to her usual tasks (lace-making). She was a unique case in that her confessors were never spiritual directors, a task that Our Lord wanted to keep for himself. Jesus made her hear his voice directly, training her, correcting her, reprimanding her if necessary and gradually leading her to the loftiest peaks of perfection. Luisa was wisely instructed and prepared during many years to receive the gift of the Divine Will.

The archbishop at that time, Giuseppe Bianchi Dottula (December 22, 1848-September 22, 1892), came to know of what was happening in Corato; having heard the opinion of several priests, he wished to exercise his authority and assume responsibility for this case. After mature reflection he thought it right to delegate to Luisa a special confessor, Fr. Michele De Benedictis, a splendid figure of a priest, to whom she opened every nook and cranny of her soul. Fr. Michele, a prudent priest with holy ways, imposed limits on her suffering and instructed her to do nothing without his permission. Indeed, it was Fr. Michele who ordered her to eat at least once a day, even if she immediately threw up everything she had swallowed. Luisa was to live on the Divine Will alone. It was under this priest that she received permission to stay in bed all the time as a victim of expiation. This was in 1888. Luisa remained nailed to her bed of pain, sitting there for another 59 years, until her death. It should be noted that until that time, although she had accepted her state as a victim, she had only occasionally stayed in bed, since obedience had never permitted her to stay in bed all the time. However, from New Year 1889 she was to remain there permanently.

In 1898 the new prelate, Archbishop Tommaso de Stefano (March 24, 1898 – 13 May 1906) delegated as her new confessor Fr. Gennaro Di Gennaro, who carried out this task for twenty-four years. The new confessor, glimpsing the marvels that the Lord was working in this soul, categorically ordered Luisa to put down in writing all that God's grace was working within her. None of the excuses made by the Servant of God to avoid obeying her confessor in this were to any avail. Not even her scant literary education could excuse her from obedience to her confessor. Fr. Gennaro Di Gennaro remained cold and implacable, although he knew that the poor woman had only been to elementary school. Thus on February 28, 1899, she began to write her diary, of which there are thirty-six large volumes! The last chapter was written on December 28, 1939, the day on which she was ordered to stop writing.

Her confessor, who died on September 10,1922, was succeeded by the canon, Fr. Francesco De Benedictis, who only assisted her for four years, because he died on January 30, 1926. Archbishop Giuseppe Leo (January 17, 1920- January 20,1939) delegated a young priest, Fr. Benedetto Calvi, as her ordinary confessor. He stayed with Luisa until she died, sharing all those sufferings and misunderstandings that beset the Servant of God in the last years of her life.

At the beginning of the century, our people were lucky enough to have Blessed Annibale Maria Di Francia present in Puglia. He wanted to open in Trani male and female branches of his newly founded congregation. When he heard about Luisa Piccarreta, he paid her a visit and from that time these two souls were inseparably linked by their common aims. Other famous priests also visited Luisa, such as, for example, Fr. Gennaro Braccali, the Jesuit, Fr. Eustachio Montemurro, who died in the odor of sanctity, and Fr. Ferdinando Cento, Apostolic Nuncio and Cardinal of Holy Mother Church.

Blessed Annibale became her extraordinary confessor and edited her writings, which were little by little properly examined and approved by the ecclesiastical authorities. In about 1926, Blessed Annibale ordered Luisa to write a book of memoirs of her childhood and adolescence. He published various writings of Luisa's, including the book *L'orologio della Passione,* which acquired widespread fame and was reprinted four times. On October 7, 1928, when the house of the sisters of the Congregation of Divine Zeal in Corato was ready, Luisa was taken to the convent in accordance with the wishes of Blessed Annibale. Blessed Annibale had already died in the odor of sanctity in Messina.

In 1938, a tremendous storm was unleashed upon Luisa Piccarreta: she was publicly disowned by Rome and her books were put on the Index. At the publication of the condemnation by the Holy Office, she immediately submitted to the authority of the Church.

A priest was sent from Rome by the ecclesiastical authorities, who asked her for all her manuscripts, which Luisa handed over promptly and without a fuss. Thus all her writings were hidden away in the secrecy of the Holy Office.

On October 7, 1938, because of orders from above, Luisa was obliged to leave the convent and find a new place to live. She spent the last nine years of her life in a house in Via Maddalena, a place which the elderly of Corato know well and from where, on March 8, 1947, they saw her body carried out.

Luisa's life was very modest; she possessed little or nothing. She lived in a rented house, cared for lovingly by her sister Angela and a few devout women. The little she had was not even enough to pay the rent. To support herself she worked diligently at making lace, earning from this the pittance she needed to keep her sister, since she herself needed neither clothes nor shoes. Her sustenance consisted of a few grams of food, which were prepared for her by her assistant, Rosaria Bucci. Luisa ordered nothing, desired nothing, and instantly vomited the food she swallowed. She did not look like a person near death's door, but nor did she appear perfectly healthy. Yet she was never idle, she spent her energy either in her daily suffering or her work, and her life, for those who knew her well, was considered a continuous miracle.

Her detachment from any payments that did not come from her daily work was marvelous! She firmly refused money and the various presents offered to her on any pretext. She never accepted money for the publication of her books. Thus one day she told Blessed Annibale that she wanted to give him the money from her author's royalties: *"I have no right to it, because what is written there is not mine"* (cf. Preface of the *L'orologio della Passione,* Messina, 1926). She scornfully refused and returned the money that pious people sometimes sent her.

Luisa's house was like a monastery, not to be entered by any curious person. She was always surrounded by a few women who lived according to her own spirituality, and by several girls who came to her house to learn lace-making. Many religious vocations emerged from this "upper room". However, her work of formation was not limited to girls alone, many young men were also sent by her to various religious institutes and to the priesthood.

Her day began at about 5.00 a.m., when the priest came to the house to bless it and to celebrate Holy Mass. Either her confessor officiated, or some delegate of his: a privileged granted by Leo XIII and confirmed by St. Pius X in 1907. After Holy Mass, Luisa would remain in prayer and thanksgiving for about two hours. At about 8.00 a.m. she would begin her work which she continued until midday; after her frugal lunch she would stay alone in her room in meditation. In the afternoon – after several hours of work – she would recite the holy Rosary. In the evening, towards 8.00 p.m., Luisa would begin to write her diary; at about midnight she would fall asleep. In the morning she would be found immobile, rigid, huddled up on her bed, her head turned to the right, and the intervention of priestly authority would be necessary to recall her to her daily tasks and allow her to sit up in bed.

Luisa died at the age of eighty-one years, ten months and nine days, on March 4, 1947, after a fortnight of illness, the only one diagnosed in her life, a bad attack of pneumonia. She died at the end of the night, at the same hour when every day the priest's blessing had freed her from her state of rigidity. Archbishop Francesco Petronelli (May 25, 1939-June 16, 1947) archbishop at the time. Luisa remained sitting up in bed. It was impossible to lay her out and – an extraordinary phenomenon – her body never suffered *rigor mortis* and remained in the position in which it had always been.

Hardly had the news of Luisa's death spread, like a river in full spate, all the people streamed into her house and police intervention was necessary to control the crowds that flocked there day and night to visit Luisa, a woman very dear to them. A voice rang out: *"Luisa the Saint has died"*. To contain all the people who were going to see her, with the permission of the civil authorities and health officials, her body was exposed for four days with no sign of corruption. Luisa did not seem dead, she was sitting up in bed, dressed in white; it was as though she were asleep, because as has already been said, her body did not suffer *rigor mortis*. Indeed, without any effort her head could be moved in all directions, her arms raised, her hands and all her fingers bent. It was even possible to lift her eyelids and see her shining eyes that had not grown dim. Everyone believed that she was still alive, immersed in a deep sleep. A council of doctors, summoned for this purpose, declared, after attentively examining the corpse, that Luisa was truly dead and that her death should be accepted as real and not merely apparent, as everyone had imagined.

Luisa had said that she was born "upside down", and that therefore it was right that her death should be "upside down" in comparison with that of other creatures. She remained in a sitting position as she had always lived, and had to be carried to the cemetery in this position, in a coffin specially made for her with a glass front and sides, so that she could be seen by everyone, like a queen upon her throne, dressed in white with the *Fiat* on her breast. More than forty priests, the chapter and the local clergy took part in the funeral procession; the sisters took turns to carry her on their shoulders, and an immense crowd of citizens surrounded her: the streets were incredibly full; even the balconies and rooftops of the houses were swarming with people, so that the procession wound slowly onwards with great difficulty. The funeral rite of the little daughter of the Divine Will was celebrated in the main church by the entire chapter. All the people of Corato followed the body to the cemetery. Everyone tried to take home a keepsake or a flower, after having touched her body with it; a few years later, her remains were translated to the parish of Santa Maria Greca.

On November 20, 1994, on the Feast of Christ the King, in the main church, Archbishop Carmelo Cassati, in the presence of a large crowd including foreign representatives, officially opened the Cause of Beatification of the Servant of God, Luisa Piccarreta.

Important dates

1865 – Luisa Piccarreta was born on April 23, the Sunday after Easter, in Corato, Bari, to Nicola Vito and Rosa Tarantino, who had five daughters: Maria, Rachele, Filomena, Luisa and Angela. A few hours after Luisa's birth, her father wrapped her in a blanket and took her to the main church for baptism. Her mother had not suffered the pangs of labor: her birth was painless.

1872 – She received Jesus in the Eucharist on the Sunday after Easter, and the sacrament of Confirmation was administered to her on that same day by Archbishop Giuseppe Bianchi Dottula of Trani.

1883 – At the age of eighteen, from the balcony of her house, she saw Jesus, bent beneath the weight of the Cross, who said to her: "*O soul! Help me!*". From that moment, solitary soul that she was, she lived in continuous union with the ineffable sufferings of her Divine Bridegroom.

1888 – She became a Daughter of Mary and a Dominican Tertiary with the name of Sr. Maddalena

1885-1947 – A chosen soul, a seraphic bride of Christ, humble and devout, whom God had endowed with extraordinary gifts, an innocent victim, a lightening conductor of Divine Justice, bedridden for sixty-two years without interruption, she was a herald of the Kingdom of the Divine Will.

March 4 – Full of merits, in the eternal light of the Divine Will she ended her days as she had lived them, to triumph with the angels and saints in the eternal splendor of the Divine Will.

March 7 – For four days her mortal remains were exposed for the veneration of an immense throng of the faithful who went to her house to have a last look at Luisa the Saint, so dear to their hearts. The funeral was a realm triumph; Luisa passed like a queen, borne aloft on shoulders among the lines of people. All the clergy, secular and religious, accompanied Luisa's body. The funeral liturgy took place in the main church with the participation of the entire chapter. In the afternoon, Luisa was buried in the family Chapel of the Calvi family.

July 3, 1963 – Her mortal remains were definitively laid to rest in Santa Maria Greca.

November 20, 1994 – Feast of Christ the King: Archbishop Carmelo Cassati officially opened the Beatification Cause of the Servant of God Luisa Piccarreta in the principal church of Corato, in the presence of a huge crowd of people, locals and foreigners.

2005 – Archbishop Giovanni Battista Picchierri, current Archbishop of Trani. It is he who requested that the Cause of Beatification of the Servant of God Luisa Piccarreta be continued.

ARCHDIOCESE

Trani – Barletta – Bisceglie – Nazareth

70059 TRANI – VIA BELTRANI, 9 – TEL.0883-583498

Trani: June 4, 2005

COMUNIQUE

The "Divine Will" has guided the Archdiocese, in this last decade, for the completion of the works regarding the process of the Cause of Beatification of the Servant of God Luisa Piccarreta. The Diocesan Postulation announces having completed this journey. It communicates that on the days of the 27th, 28th, and 29th of October 2005 it will celebrate the 2nd International Congress with the conclusion of the diocesan process.

The Pious Association Luisa Piccarreta Little Children of the Divine Will*, in Corato, has been charged with performing the job of Secretary for the celebration and welcome of guests. Later the program of the celebration will be published in a definitive way.

May Jesus Christ present in the Eucharist guide us as He has guided His Servant Luisa.

The Vicar General

(His Grace Mons. Savino Giannotti)

COME HOLY SPIRIT, COME SUPREME WILL,

DOWN TO REIGN IN YOUR KINGDOM ON EARTH

AND IN OUR HEARTS!

COME HOLY SPIRIT, COME SUPREME WILL,

DOWN TO REIGN IN YOUR KINGDOM ON EARTH

AND IN OUR HEARTS!

COME HOLY SPIRIT, COME SUPREME WILL,

DOWN TO REIGN IN YOUR KINGDOM ON EARTH AND IN OUR HEARTS!